Friendship

STUDIES IN SOCIOLOGY

Series Editor, Professor W. M. Williams, University of Swansea

The aim of this series is to provide essential surveys of key concepts in sociology. Each book will review the present state of the art, identify major issues and problems, and examine possible solutions and future avenues of research.

Other titles in the series include:

Friendship
DEVELOPING A SOCIOLOGICAL PERSPECTIVE

GRAHAM ALLAN MA, PhD
Senior Lecturer in Sociology, University of Southampton

WESTVIEW PRESS
Boulder & San Francisco

Published in 1989 in London by
Harvester Wheatsheaf,
66 Wood Lane End, Hemel Hempstead,
Hertfordshire, HP2 4RG
A division of
Simon & Schuster International Group

Published in 1989 in the United States by
Westview Press
5500 Central Avenue
Boulder, Colorado 80301

Printed and bound in Great Britain by Billings and Sons Ltd, Worcester

Library of Congress Cataloging-in-Publication Data

Allan, Graham A.
Friendship: a sociological perspective/Graham Allan.
p.   cm.
Includes bibliographical references.
ISBN 0-8133-1036-9. –– ISBN 0-8133-1037-7 (pbk.)
1. Friendship –– sociological aspects.   I. Title.
HM132.5.A44   1989   89-38994
302.3'4 –– dc20   CIP

1 2 3 4 5 93 92 91 90 89

For Sue, Christopher and Peter

124024

CONTENTS

ACKNOWLEDGEMENTS

Many people have encouraged me in the writing of this book. I owe much to my colleagues in the Department of Sociology and Social Policy at Southampton University, both for their general interest and, more specifically, for carrying many of my teaching and other responsibilities while I was on study leave. The Department has also funded my attendance at a number of conferences where some of the ideas discussed in this book were first presented. I owe a special thanks to Glynis Evans for re-typing much of this book for me. I would also like to thank Graham Crow for commenting on the full draft of the text and Rebecca Adams for her comments on Chapter 6. Thanks are also due to Jacques Coenen-Huther. Discussing his Swiss research on friendship played an important part in stimulating my own thoughts and encouraged me to start writing this book. Other friends and colleagues contributed directly or indirectly to the book – though not all knew it at the time! Finally, special thanks go to Susan Allan, as well as Richard, Nicola, Christopher and Peter, who made sure that the demands of the book were kept in some sort of perspective. She knows what I mean.

1

SOCIOLOGICAL QUESTIONS AND THE SOCIOLOGY OF FRIENDSHIP

There are many theories which assert that modern culture is one in which alienation and isolation are to be expected as the normal state of affairs. With the wide-ranging economic and social changes that industrialisation generated, life is reputed to have become more individualised, privatised and, in many ways, more selfish. Yet at an everyday level our commitment to, fascination with and interest in personal relationships of all forms show no sign of waning. The popularity of soap operas on television and of novels that essentially revolve around domestic and personal intrigue provides one index of this. More important, though, we also devote a great deal of time and effort to managing our own relationships and perhaps only slightly less to gossiping about other people's.

Personal relationships, of course, take a variety of forms. Outside the family itself, friendship appears to be one relationship to which we attach special importance personally and culturally. Not only do our friends help to provide us with our sense of identity, but they also confirm our social worth. Thus, we tend to think of people with lots of friends as most likely to be happy and those without as often lonely and unfortunate. The value of friendship is also indicated by the popularity of books and magazine articles giving hints and advice on how to make and keep friends.

Yet despite its significance in our everyday life, the topic of friendship has received rather little attention from sociologists. There has been relatively little serious analysis of friendship as a form of personal relationship occurring in industrialised societies (Hess, 1979). Instead, friendship is treated as being rather peripheral to the core structural properties of economic and social relations in developed capitalist societies. It is seen as an extra, as something that adds a little flavour to social life, but which of itself is relatively unimportant in the nitty-gritty of economic and social organisation. In other words, in a somewhat unsociological fashion, friendship is taken to be essentially a personal matter, rather than one which has any social interest or consequence. It is as though many sociologists have accepted uncritically the conventional definition of friendship as a freely chosen, voluntary and predominantly expressive relationship (Cohen and Rajkowski, 1982). As a result, they have often not sought to look behind this idealised portrayal and so have failed to recognise the social significance and value of friendship ties (Seiden and Bart, 1976). If, as this definition asserts, friendship is just a matter of personal attraction and choice, how can it be of relevance to a discipline concerned with constraint and structure?

Certainly, the dominant traditions within the discipline do not encourage an interest in friendship. Friendship seems well removed from concerns like stratification, economic development and political consciousness which have tended to be seen as the 'real' subject matter of the discipline. Equally, the classic writers, with their interest in the transformation that industrial capitalism was generating in social and economic life, paid little heed to ties of amity and cooperation, except in glancing back at the ways of the previous era. Only (the now rather unread) Simmel and Tonnies of the early sociologists devoted much of their work to an explicit analysis of forms of sociability and how these were patterned by social conditions. Yet, on reflection, it is clear that ties of association and solidarity are undoubtedly relevant to some of the issues that concerned the early generations of sociologists. For example, Marx's analysis of class conflict and the creation of class consciousness through collective involvement in capitalist production, Weber's understanding of status within systems of stratification, and Durkheim's concerns with the forms of commitment and solidarity that tie individuals to the social formation all point in some fashion to the relevance of patterns of friendship and other associational bonds to traditional sociological interests.

Similarly, many more recent empirical studies of different aspects of social and economic life have, in fact, made some sort of reference to ties of friendship, though few of them treat these relationships as a major issue. For example, community studies normally include some analysis of the level of social integration found in their locality, using friendship as well as kinship and neighbourhood solidarity as an indication of this Mogey, 1956; (Littlejohn, 1963; Stacey *et al.*, 1975). Studies of organisations – bureaucracies, schools, factories, etc. – have also often pointed to the way in which informal relations of a friendship type help to oil the more formal channels of communication and command, thereby enabling individuals to achieve or counter the organisation's goals as suits their interests (Crozier, 1964; Willis, 1977; Westwood, 1984; Litwak, 1985). Equally, research into personal crises – for example, unemployment, divorce or bereavement – has been concerned with the role played by friends at these times, as well as with the impact these events have on the patterns of friendship maintained (Hart, 1976; Bankoff, 1981; Morris, 1984).

Many other examples of studies in which friendship is relevant, though not focal, could be cited. The point is simply that friendship of itself is not without interest or salience to sociology as a discipline. Yet, notwithstanding such important contributions as those by Fischer *et al.* (1977), Hess (1972; 1979), Jerrome (1984) and Wellman (1985) amongst others, no fully-fledged sociology of friendship has really developed. Indeed, generally, when friendship is the topic of study, it tends to be viewed in isolation from the types of social process and action mentioned above and, as a consequence, to be treated in a rather idealised way. In other words, it is usually not integrated into an analysis with any wider empirical or theoretical significance, but in a distinctly asociological fashion just examined for its own sake.

Two related features of friendship as found in our culture help to account for the rather isolated way in which friendship patterns are analysed in friendship research. The first concerns the problem of defining the subject matter of such research. What exactly is a friend? What characteristics does a relationship need to have to warrant being termed a friendship? How wide are the criteria? The problem here is that unlike the case of kin or neighbour or colleague relationships, there are no 'external' grounds for characterising someone as a friend. What matters is the nature of the relationship they have with you, rather than their position *vis-à-vis* you in some independent domain. So, for example, while it is relatively straightforward to specify all the kin known to you, in many ways it is harder to separate those who are friends from those who are not, as the boundary between the categories is not clearly defined.

Perhaps more important from the perspective of empirical research based on interviewing, the researcher is faced with the problem of knowing whether or not his or her respondents are all using equivalent notions of what friendship is when providing data about their friendships. Often the result is that researchers concentrate on close or best friends in analysing friendship patterns, but as a consequence fail to investigate the full range of those who in one context or another fall under the umbrella of friendship. Equally, because their concern is with best friends, i.e., those who most closely approximate the cultural ideals of friendship, the resultant analyses tend to concentrate on the internal properties of these ties, rather than on the way in which friendship in a more general sense is integrated into the day-to-day routines of social and economic life.

A second related reason why friendship studies have tended to isolate friendship from wider social processes stems from the fact that friendship itself is not institutionalised in any real sense in our society (Paine, 1969; Hess, 1979; Matthews, 1986). So, for example, in contrast to the practice in some other societies, friendship is not usually celebrated in any formal fashion. There are no rituals associated with it nor any specifically public affirmation of the solidarity that exists between those who are friends.

While there are certainly norms and conventions which pattern friends' behaviour towards one another (Suttles, 1970), friendship of itself is not seen as being incorporated into the institutional framework of the society in the way that, say, kinship is. As a result, when sociologists have studied friendship they have not really asked 'institutionally oriented' questions of the sort that are routine in other areas of the discipline. Thus, whereas the sociology of the family has long asked about the effects of industrialisation on family life, or about the way in which kin ties are used by families and individuals to further their material interests, the sociology of friendship has been curiously unconcerned with these and equivalent issues. Instead, as discussed above, the questions posed have been predominantly at an individual level, rather than being about the social consequences or significance of the way an individual is integrated with others through the range of ties that can be subsumed under a more or less loose definition of friendship.

The fact that friendship is not institutionalised is itself an issue of some sociological interest, as in some ways it makes the relationship rather special. Certainly, not all societies foster or tolerate the freedom and flexibility that, at one level, friendship in our society involves (Jerrome, 1984). To begin with, some societies simply do not recognise a form of personal relationship equivalent to our tie of friendship. In these societies personal commitment is channelled through kinship and locality, so that when people become close the tie is understood in terms of these domains rather than of friendship *per se*. In other societies, ties of friendship may be recognised, but be seen as needing quite firm and explicit social control. This may be achieved through the use of ceremony and ritual which serve to acknowledge the relationship socially, thereby marking it off as special and, in some cases, formalising it to the extent that appropriate behaviour is quite rigidly delineated and specified. Such institutionalised patterns of friendship contrast markedly with the freedom inherent in our cultural idea of friendship (Banton, 1966; Leyton, 1974).

Comparing the patterns of interpersonal relationships found in other societies with those occurring in developed capitalist ones suggests interesting questions about the way that friendship is organised in our society, questions which by and large have concerned anthropologists rather more than sociologists. For example, what is it in our social and economic structure that allows non-institutionalised personal relationships to develop? Why do these relationships apparently not need the force of social control? What type of social control is exercised over them? More generally, what role does friendship play in our society? What social and economic functions does it fulfil? While these more structural questions are more frequently posed by anthropologists than by sociologists, they are clearly of central importance to an adequate sociology of friendship.

The point here is that all too often sociologists analysing friendship have focused solely on the personal qualities of friendship – on issues like why people are attracted to one another or on the nature of their feelings for each other – rather than on more structural issues. As suggested above, anthropologists have been far more concerned with such structural matters. For example, anthropologists (Barnes, 1954; Bott, 1957) were the first to develop network analysis as a way of examining how the structure of the full set of informal relationships an individual maintained influenced his or her behaviour. Much of the more interesting work in this field continued to be done by anthropologists (Mitchell, 1969; Boissevain and Mitchell, 1973). At a different level, anthropologists' concern with more structural aspects of friendships and other informal ties is demonstrated by their interest in what, following Wellman (1985), can loosely be termed the 'political economy' of informal relations. Far more than sociologists, they have sought to analyse the various ways in which people use their informal relationships for solving the different problems that face them at an everyday level and in manipulating their way through the more formal organisational constraints that confront them (Burridge, 1957; Pitt-Rivers, 1961; Boissevain, 1974; Leyton, 1974). At a more general level still, there is the implicitly comparative approach, referred to earlier, which poses questions about the forms of friendship that the social and economic structures of different societies permit and facilitate (Cohen, 1961; Wolf, 1966; Paine, 1970; Brain, 1976). As stated, not all cultures allow the development of relationships equivalent to the friendships we take to be almost natural.

The fact that anthropologists have shown more interest than sociologists in analysing the role of friendship within social structures is not coincidental. As a discipline, anthropology has focused far more on the patterning of personal relationships within a society and on the way this patterning helps sustain the dominant social institutions and practices than sociology ever has done. This is most evident in anthropologists' commitment to the study of kinship as a means of uncovering the mechanisms of social order in the type of non-industrialised societies they have traditionally studied. This concern is no longer solely a consequence of the social institutions within such societies often being formally premised upon principles of kinship, but has come to be one of the main parameters of the discipline, just as the study of stratification is within sociology. As some anthropologists shifted their attention to more industrialised, western societies where kinship is far less integrated into social and economic organisation, they maintained their interest in the interplay between social institutions, on the one hand, and the patterns of personal relationships that developed. However, as kinship is so much less integrated into social and economic life in these latter societies other informal ties, like those of friendship, patronage, and clientship, received relatively greater attention.

In addition to the substantive concerns of the discipline, the research methods most favoured by anthropologists also encourage a specific interest in the social characteristics and form of personal relationships. In the study of unfamiliar small-scale, non-literate societies, some form of participant observation offers obvious methodological advantages. As with the focus on kinship, this methodology almost became built into the parameters of the discipline and was transferred into new fields as anthropologists began to apply their expertise to the study of advanced capitalist societies. While different sorts of survey are now regularly used in anthropology, participant observation continues to be the main method used by anthropologists to uncover social reality. This, together with the continuing tendency within the discipline to concentrate analysis on specific and relatively bounded settings – a work place, a locality or whatever – has meant that anthropologists studying industrialised society are well-placed to recognise the ways in which informal relationships contribute to the social fabric. Participant observation, and the rather holistic appreciation of settings it encourages, enables a social analyst not simply to see the more formal, more public institutionalised patterns of behaviour, but also to get behind this and uncover the mortar that holds these patterns together. It is this capacity to focus on the details of how informal relationships operate in particular contexts, and relate these to more large-scale, structural features of the social environment that has made the anthropology of such relationships so much more fertile than sociological perspectives.

The fact is that, in contrast to anthropologists, sociologists have relied far more on interviewing than on observation for obtaining information on friendships. Moreover, their concern with representative sampling and statistical generalisation has often resulted in their interviewing techniques being highly structured and standardised, especially in North American studies. There is, of course, nothing inherently wrong in collecting data through interviews on a topic like friendship, where the individual's understanding of the character of his or her relationships is a component element of the subject matter. However, over-reliance on relatively standardised interviews has rather limited sociological accounts of friendship in two respects.

First, interviewing in general, but more structured interviewing especially, individualises responses and makes it quite difficult to locate the described behaviour within its interactive context, not least because the account is necessarily one-sided. One consequence of this constraint is that much friendship research is, in effect, 'psychologised'. The information collected is concerned with feeling states, with the personal significance of friendships, with the level and type of emotional support obtained from friends, as well as with basic sociographic data on such things as the number of friends a person has, where they live and how often they are seen.

Secondly, there is a sense in which this form of data collection generates information about the ideology of friendship, rather than about the way that friendship actually is. In other words, the description of friendships proffered in more formal interview settings are likely to be influenced by cultural notions of the way friendships should be. As with marriage, what may be obtained are 'public' accounts of friendship, rather than more truthful 'private' accounts (Cornwell, 1984). Of itself, such a tendency is likely to make it harder to get behind ideologically tinged portrayals of friendship and to collect information on what was referred to above as the political economy of friendship.

The argument here, then, is that many sociological studies of friendship fail to locate friendships adequately within the broader social structures in which they occur. The questions they ask tend not to be focused on such matters, in part as a result of the type of methodology frequently used in them. Naturally, this applies to some areas of the sociology of friendship more than others. One area of the subject where it is noticeable that attempts are made to place friendship patterns within a wider context is in gerontology. A number of researchers have illustrated how the elderly's friendships are shaped by their social circumstances, both now and over the course of their lives (Jerrome, 1984; Matthews, 1986; Adams, 1987). Aside from gerontology, though, much of the more interesting writing on friendship has come from analyses that do not take such relationships as their focus. For example, recent work on unemployment, on divorce and on the (so-called) informal economy have not only provided interesting information on the way in which patterns of informal social integration alter with social circum-stances, but have also indicated contextually, rather than, as it were, abstractly, the claims that can be made on different types of relationship (Hart, 1976; Binns and Mars, 1984; Pahl, 1984; Morris, 1984; McKee and Bell, 1986).

The intention of this book is to try to integrate some of the research material that there is on friendship, so as to encourage a more satisfactory sociology of friendship than has, in my view, developed so far. A major aim will be to show that friendship is not simply the voluntary and socially marginal relationship it is often taken to be. Following Elias's (1973) injunction, the task of sociology is taken to be that of showing how people's choices and actions are constrained by the social structures in which they occur. This applies to friendship as it does to other spheres. The sociology of friendship needs to come out of the 'voluntaristic twilight' in which it is currently shrouded (Elias, 1973, p. xvii). This means not just asking what limits the friendship choices open to people, but also asking how their friendships are related to other aspects of their lives. As discussed above, it is not satisfactory to treat friendship in isolation as just a personal, voluntary relationship that provides psychological support. The essence of sociology is structure, constraint and the relationship between the elements that make up the whole. In much the same way as the sociology of the family has developed over the last twenty years to analyse the significance, rather than the supposed marginality of family life, so this book will pose questions about the social relevance of friendship and the role it plays within the wider social structure.

It is worth emphasising at the outset that the book will not provide definitive answers to these questions. It is in many ways just a beginning – an attempt to set an appropriate agenda, rather than provide absolute solutions. Its purpose is to argue for a sociological analysis of friendship and indicate ways in which this might proceed. Thus, essentially the book should be seen as an introduction to the subject and as an attempt to draw together some of the more interesting issues that have emerged from recent sociological research concerned with friendship, in both Britain and the United States. The book does not contain any new empirical findings, but is more a text that attempts to build on other people's research. However, as would be expected from the above, it is a selective text, rather than one which seeks to provide students and others with a résumé of all the research recently published about the topic. In the main, the studies referred to in it are included because of their relevance to the central concern of the book: the relationship between friendship and other aspects of the social structure. If nothing else, it is hoped that the book will persuade readers that there is a sociological dimension to friendship and encourage students to undertake research into what is undoubtedly an underdeveloped area within the discipline.

THE PLAN OF THE BOOK

Chapter 2 will be concerned with examining the concept of friendship and the various meanings attached to it. The argument will be that the usual narrow definitions of friendship are not particularly helpful for a sociological analysis of its significance. Because the relationship is varied, and because it is not institutionalised, the full range of relationships that in different contexts may be referred to as friendships needs to be considered and the differences within them examined. In particular, it is not sufficient to focus, as many studies do, on close or best friends, as there is ample reason to regard these as a rather unrepresentative sub-set of friendship overall. For purposes of analysis, the notion of friendship needs to be extended so as to include workmates, acquaintances and others who may not always be specified as friends. In one sense, what is involved here is an analysis of social integration generally, for only against such a relatively full background of sociability is it possible to interpret and locate friendship properly.

Chapter 3 will examine structural influences on friendship. It will focus on the ways in which opportunities for sociability are patterned and the degree to which these opportunities are of a form that allows friendships to be developed and serviced. The argument will be that friendship is not just a matter of free choice and selection, but that the availability of friends is a consequence of people's location within the social structure. Furthermore, what one does with these friends and the use made of them is also patterned by these same social factors. In other words, the thrust of this chapter is that a person's friendships should not be viewed just as a set of voluntary relationships, as much of the psychologically oriented literature especially tends to do, but as ties which are at least in part shaped and constrained by the configuration of social and material conditions which characterise an individual's life. Issues like domestic situation, gender, work patterns, geographical location, social mobility and the like collectively play some role in structuring the extent and nature of friendships.

Chapter 4 will be concerned with examining the social significance of friendship. Building on the earlier discussion, it will examine the way in which friendships are routinely used in social life and the part they play in helping people cope with and meet the demands that are made of them. The emphasis will not be on the psychological or emotional support that friends give, though this will not be ignored, but more on the way in which friendships are incorporated into social organisation, their social utility and their significance for social identity. The argument will be that, just as the family is not peripheral to non-domestic matters, as the standard functionalist thesis tended to imply, neither is friendship totally separate from other concerns, in the rather idealistic way that much of the existing literature implicitly treats it.

Chapter 5 will examine the relationship between gender and friendship. As well as augmenting arguments made earlier about the way in which gender differences shape opportunities for developing and servicing friendships, the chapter will examine the extent to which males and females construct different friendship patterns, make different use of their friends and come to expect different things from them. The reasons for these differences will be analysed, drawing on some of the issues raised in the previous chapters. Though the chapter will contain some discussion of childhood friendships, the emphasis will be on the way in which the material and social circumstances of the genders affect the patterning of friendship in adult life. The chapter will also spend some time looking at cross-gender friendships. Although there is relatively little research on these relationships, they are of special interest, both because of their potential or actual sexual element and because, in some respects, they contravene the norm that friendship is a tie between social equals.

Chapter 6 will analyse the significance of friendship in later life. Arguably, this is the topic that has been most adequately researched by sociologists of friendship, in that a number of studies exist which are concerned with the social significance of friendship for the elderly. More than most, these studies attempt a structural analysis of friendship by examining the role that friends play in their respondents' routine lives. The chapter will review this research and argue that friendship does not become less salient with age, as some models of ageing imply. However, this does not mean that friendship behaviour does not alter. On the contrary, in line with the arguments developed in earlier chapters, changes in the elderly's social and material circumstances will be reflected in the patterning of their friendships. Especially amongst the 'young elderly', this can entail a growth of friendship circles, rather than any demise. The focus in the final part of this chapter will be on widowhood. As before, the purpose of this section will be to show how the friendships of widows are influenced by their social situation.

Chapter 7 will be concerned with friendship and change. It will examine the consequences for friendship patterns of crises and other major social events in people's lives. It will provide an opportunity to see how friends are used to help cope with such things as divorce, unemployment, domestic violence, and the provision of care for those in need. The argument will be that, contrary to the romantic ideals of friendship popularly asserted, the majority of friendships provide only short-term assistance. In the longer run, an individual's friendships are likely to alter and be replaced by others when his or her social position changes significantly. The chapter will argue that there is nothing untoward about this, but that it is a consequence of the way in which friendship is socially constructed. Within the context of the book, it is an important aspect of friendship, for it indicates both the limitations there are in most friendships and the extent to which friendship is patterned by social, rather than individual, factors.

Chapter 8 will be concerned with exploring how social class affects the organisation of informal relationships. Building on the discussions contained in Chapters 2 and 3 , and on previous analyses in the research literature on friendship, the chapter will explore how the form or style of friendship which people develop is influenced by their social and economic circumstances. In contrast to Chapter 3, which is concerned with the opportunities individuals have to create and service friendships and other informal ties, this chapter will examine how those relationships an individual actually does have are typically organised and the boundaries which are placed around them. It will seek to explain the class variations there are in friendship patterns by locating them within a broader context. As well as examining economic and material influences, the chapter will discuss how the pattern of marriage and the organisation of the home influence the form that informal relationships of a friendship type take.

The final chapter will present a summary of the different strands of argument developed in the rest of the book. It will spell out what the main characteristics of a sociology of friendship are and indicate how these differ from the psychology of friendship which currently dominates the social science literature. In providing an overview, it will show how friendship ties, in whatever guise they take, need to be placed within a broader structural context if they are to be understood properly. The chapter will conclude by discussing ways in which the sociology of friendship could usefully be developed in the future.

2

FRIENDS, MATES AND OTHERS

C. S. Lewis (1960) characterises friendship as one of four great forms of love. While such a claim strikes a strange chord for many more used to contemporary notions of love, in which sexual and romantic connotations dominate, he is merely following a tradition whose roots can be traced back beyond Aristotle. It is a tradition which continues to interest moral philosophers and theologians to the present day. The concern of such thinkers is almost invariably with the highest ideals of friendship and with what they take to be its fullest and most complete form: 'genuine', 'real' or 'true' friendships. In these ideal friendships, the solidarity of the friends, based solely on their personal and voluntary commitment to each other, is taken to be unfettered by any selfish or instrumental concerns. Each gives what the other needs, without thought to cost or reward, simply because of the fact of their friendship. From this perspective, such friendship can be recognised as a bond of enormous moral significance: as one of the highest expressions of voluntary, altruistic commitment there can be between people (Brain, 1976).

From a sociological viewpoint, such a portrayal of friendship is certainly extreme. It is an idealised formulation which, while serving the purposes of moral philosophy, is less adequate as a description of friendships as they routinely occur. Nonetheless, the values that are expressed in it are ones which, within limits, are generally held in high esteem. While our culture accepts that precedence should normally be given to family members, especially to one's spouse and children, loyalty and commitment to close friends is taken to be a moral virtue. However, the culture is equally clear that such forms of extensive solidarity are rather rare and cannot normally be expected of run-of-the-mill friendships. Indeed, those individuals who have in some way demonstrated a greater loyalty and altruism are often distinguished from ordinary friends by the use of prefixes like 'real' or 'true'. These are the friendships which have either lasted for a particularly long period and survived major changes in the circumstances of the friends, or ones which have provided an especially high level of support during some period of personal crisis (Allan, 1979; Maines, 1981; Matthews, 1983). Because such friendships seem to those involved to be virtually inalienable, and because they each know they can rely on the other to provide whatever support is possible in times of need, they approximate most closely to the form of friendship portrayed in philosophical discussion.

However, it is important to recognise that such friendships are few and far between. Most people have, at most, one or two friendships that they would characterise as 'real' or 'true', and certainly the great majority of acknowledged friendships are not of this type. Moreover, such friendships often differ from other friendships in being less, rather than more, active. That is, those who regard each other as 'real' or 'true' friends do not necessarily see one another very frequently, nor do very much together. This seeming paradox is, in fact, inherent in the very idea of this type of friendship, for circumstances – such as living some distance apart – which make regular interaction difficult to arrange and which would result in the gradual demise of other friendships, do not threaten these relationships. Indeed, the fact that they can survive such contingencies serves to demonstrate their special quality.

While it is true that 'real' friendships represent something of the cultural, as well as the philosophical, ideal, the most significant fact about them from a sociological perspective is that they are not typical. Indeed, it could be argued that there is no one typical form of friendship, but rather a variety or range of relationships which combine in different ways the various elements that are entailed in the general notion of friendship. This is so, not just in straightforward behavioural terms – how often and where friends meet; who else is present; what type and range of activities are undertaken, etc., – important though these are, but also with respect to such things as the level of intimacy, trust and commitment entailed. In Paine's (1969) terms, there can be a good deal of variation in the 'rules of relevancy' of different friendships. What is taken to be pertinent to one friendship may not play any part in another. To draw on Bates's (1964) more graphic analogy of the self as a house with various rooms in it, different friends may be allowed to see into different rooms at different times or to venture into them in a different order. As important is the fact that not all friends will ever be allowed to view the whole house. 'Real' friends may at some time have seen it all, but there will never be any intention that others become as intimate as this.

The analogy is not perfect, but it serves to make the point that friendships do differ and that not all are aiming for the peak of the philosopher's 'true' friendship. Other forms occur and are valued in their own right. In other words, different 'boundaries' are constructed around friendships. These boundaries, which can be conceived of as representing the implicit limits of friends' involvement, knowledge and intimacy with each other, are not necessarily fixed, though in some relationships they may in practice remain quite static for considerable periods of time. In the majority of friendships, however, the boundary constructed around each relationship is liable to shift with time, in line with changes in the circumstances and interests of those involved. The boundaries drawn around different relationships will also vary in their degree of permeability. The parameters of some will be quite rigidly delineated, with certain topics and issues never being discussed nor considered relevant. In others, there will be greater flexibility and tolerance over the matters that can be broached.

To a large extent the location of the boundaries that characterise different friendships is determined by personal choice and preference. What friends wish to do and discuss with each other is a matter of tacit negotiation and agreement between them as their relationship unfurls. However, as will be discussed in greater depth in Chapter 3, the 'decisions' they come to will be influenced by the constellation of factors that impinges on and patterns their immediate social environment and determines the space in their lives for sociability. Furthermore, cultural and sub-cultural conventions about the way in which ties of friendship and sociability are normally fashioned will also affect the nature of the boundaries that are drawn around some of these relationships. This is a matter which will be returned to and developed more fully in a later section of this chapter.

Not only does the 'content' of friendships vary, but variation can also occur in the actual labels given to these relationships. As implied above, those relationships which are categorised as 'true' or 'real' friendships will certainly be termed friendships, as will others which more or less closely approximate to them. However, other relationships which have elements in common with these friendships may or may not be recognised and termed friendships, depending both on context and content. Thus, someone may be referred to as a friend in one setting, but not in another – 'Well I've known him a while, but I don't suppose he's really a friend.' More important, some friend-like relationships may be referred to by other terms such as 'pal', 'mate', 'mucker' or 'buddy'. On some occasions such terms may just reflect different linguistic practices, but equally in some instances they are used to express more adequately the nature of relationships which, for one reason or another, do not seem to fit so well under the rubric of 'friend'.

In many ways, this is the nub of the problem. As mentioned in Chapter 1, the concept of 'friend' does not serve simply to represent those with whom you have a sociable relationship, in the way that the term 'neighbour' indicates someone you live close to, or 'kin' someone you are related to through blood or marriage. Rather, the term 'friend' also denotes something about the quality of the relationship you have with that person. In other words, 'friend' is not just a categorical label, like 'colleague' or 'cousin', indicating the social position of each individual relative to the other. Rather, it is a relational term which signifies something about the quality and character of the relationship involved. You can be on good, bad or indifferent terms with a neighbour. That person remains a neighbour simply as a consequence of residential propinquity. To characterise someone as a friend is clearly a rather different exercise, for here the characterisation is highly dependent on the nature of the relationship.

At one level, this would appear to simplify the analysis of friend relationships. As the character of these ties is built into their specification, relatively little effort would seem needed to uncover their content. In fact, though, it acts the other way and creates greater difficulties because of the lack of precision there is about the defining criteria of friendship (Maines, 1981). While there are boundary problems with categorical labels like 'kin' or 'neighbour' – is someone who lives in the next street a neighbour? Is a second cousin once removed part of your kin? – these are relatively minor in comparison with the problems of designating friends, for, as discussed above, the criteria of friendship are both imprecise and variable by context. As a result, people may not only use the label in different ways at different times, but also some relationships which meet some of the criteria of friendship may not be labelled in this way because they do not meet them all (Cohen and Rajkowski, 1982).

The issues this raises for the sociological analysis of friendship patterns will be discussed in a later section. First, it is necessary to disentangle the various elements that the notion of friendship entails so that the field of study can be adequately specified.

CHARACTERISTICS OF FRIENDSHIP

Friendship is frequently defined in the research literature as a voluntary, informal and personal relationship (Paine, 1969; McCall, 1970; Jerrome, 1984). These elements are certainly important within the cultural conception of what friendship is, but they are not exhaustive, nor are they as clear-cut as they seem (Cohen and Rajkowski, 1982).

There can be little dispute that friendship is a voluntary relationship. With the possible exception of young children, no one is forced into friendship. More than is the case with most relationships in which people are involved, they are ties which are chosen quite freely and which can be ended as desired. Certainly, any relationship which is felt to be imposed either by circumstances or by other people is not likely to be described as one of friendship. However, as will be discussed in the next chapter, friendship is a little less free than it sometimes appears, as there are clear social, and for that matter physical, limitations on opportunities and eligibility for friendship. Moreover, some friendships continue not just because those involved purposefully wish them to do so, but because, in some sense, it is easier for them to continue than for them to end. For instance, some friendships are maintained because those involved keep meeting each other in sociable, i.e., 'friendship relevant', settings or because they are both bound into a relatively closed network with other friends.

In a similar way, friendship is, without doubt, an informal and personal relationship. It is not one which is predicated on membership of or participation in some formal association or organisation, nor one in which there are set rules that have to be followed if others are to perform their tasks satisfactorily. It is not, in other words, a relationship that is embedded structurally, in the sense of being a component element of some wider social formation which depends for its success on the performance of the friends. As discussed in Chapter 1, the relationship is not institutionalised, but is more free-floating, with its content and 'shape' being a matter for determination by the friends, rather than by any external influence

(Suttles, 1970). Yet, as with the apparent voluntariness of the tie, the informal and personal character of friendships is not as absolute as it seems in the idealised abstract. To begin with, many friendships originate between people who are involved with each other in formal organisations of some sort, the most common one probably being employment. As they develop, many of these friendships will become quite independent of their initial organisational base. Others, though, will become so to a much lesser extent. While, for example, those involved may occasionally meet outside this setting, most of their interaction will occur within its boundaries and be defined as consequent upon their joint participation. The extent to which they recognise their relationship as one of friendship will depend in part on the extent to which they see it as free of organisational constraint, but either way their common organisational membership provides a backcloth which has some effect in shaping their tie.

Similarly, some friendships are, as it were, group friendships; somewhat contrary to the image portrayed in most definitions of friendship, they are not one-to-one ties, but involve a number of people meeting collectively for some purpose. While some of the dyads within the group are likely to be stronger than others, the nature of the friendships – and again they may not always be labelled thus – within the group is in a sense not just a personal matter, but is shaped by what, for the want of a better term, may be called the sub-cultural norms established by the group as a whole. Again, where people are involved in a set of friendships which form part of a relatively closed network, the nature of each individual tie is likely to be influenced and, in a sense controlled, by the other ties involved and to this extent not just be a personal concern.

The intention here is not to deny that friendship is a voluntary, informal and personal relationship, but rather to argue for a degree of relativism within the definition. Certainly, relationships which are not seen as having these properties are unlikely to be regarded as friendships, but in some other ties, which are to some degree recognised as friendships, these matters may not be so clear-cut.

In addition to these factors, friendship is routinely defined as a relationship concerned principally with sociability. In that it is a voluntary tie, its main rationale is that the friends enjoy spending time with each other doing what they do. There are, of course, myriad different ways in which sociability can be organised. It covers a great number of different activities. Indeed, the same person may spend time with different friends in very different ways, each of which provides a focus for sociability. Yet, while sociability is seen as intrinsic to friendship, once again the relationship between the two is not as straightforward as it initially appears. Certainly, not all those others with whom people are sociable are regarded as friends in any very full sense. As Kurth (1970) notes, there is an important distinction between being friendly and friendship. Moreover, while those with whom one, in some sense, chooses to be sociable are likely to be recognised as friends in some fashion, the level of sociability of itself does not necessarily indicate the strength of the friendship.

In particular, a good deal of time may be spent socialising with some people in certain settings without their necessarily coming to be regarded as close friends. The sociability may be seen, as a consequence of the setting, as much as – or even more than – as a consequence of the relationship itself. So, for example, members of a sports club may spend a good deal of time at the club talking and mixing with other members. Those individuals with whom they spend most time there are likely to be regarded as friends, though not necessarily as close friends. The time spent with them may be enjoyed, they may be fun to be with, but it does not automatically follow that they will be trusted with the kind of intimate information about the self that is shared with 'true' friends. Conversely, at the other end of the scale as mentioned earlier, people who are regarded as close friends may not, in fact, be interacted with at all frequently and as a consequence may rather lose touch with the day-to-day issues that confront each other. Because of the solidarity and trust that has been generated over time, they remain close friends, but, because of circumstances, actually spend little time socialising together. The point here is that while sociability is quite central to friendship, it is neither all there is to the relationship, nor necessarily indicative of its significance.

As Lopata (1981) notes, some writers emphasise that friendship is more of an expressive than an instrumental relationship. It is not, in other words, a relationship which is generated or sustained because of any extrinsic material benefits that can accrue from it. Equally, it is not really supposed to be a relationship in which each side carefully weighs up the costs and rewards of their interaction before proceeding, in the way that happens with, say, business contracts. Certainly, few things are more likely to damage a friendship than one side's believing that the other is sustaining the friendship for purely instrumental purposes, aside, perhaps, from the explicit betrayal of trust.

However, the issue of instrumentality within friendship is, like the other matters raised here, rather more complex than this formulation allows (Paine, 1969). Indeed, an argument to be developed later in this book is the reverse of this: that friendships *are* used instrumentally; that friends regularly provide a variety of services for one another; and that these services play a larger part in the routine organisation of daily life than is normally assumed. Nonetheless, it is true that friendships must not be defined in these terms. In other words, while friends can be used to achieve a variety of objectives, their instrumentality should not be the basis or rationale for the relationship. Indeed, normally in using one another the friends are quite careful to demonstrate this. The usual way of doing so is to ensure that there is a regular give and take within the relationship so that the value of the exchanges – not just in financial terms, but also in terms of effort involved *vis-à-vis* the resources available to the friends – are broadly balanced, at least over the long run.

THE BALANCE OF FRIENDSHIP

This indicates one of the most interesting features of friendship from a sociological perspective: that friendship is essentially a relationship of equality. In other words, in addition to being informal and free from broader structural imperatives, friendship is a bond in which issues of hierarchy and authority have no bearing. Within the friendship, those who are friends treat each other as equal, even if outsiders do not, and make sure there is a general reciprocity and equivalence of exchange within their relationship. This obvious and apparently straightforward characteristic of friendship has a number of implications which are quite central to an understanding of its social significance.

While it is difficult, if not impossible, to demonstrate the transactional equivalence that exists within friendship – as the value of the exchanges is subjective and often intrinsic – it is evident that friends make a good deal of effort to ensure that they are not abusing their friendship by taking too much without reciprocating. This becomes quite apparent when some monetary value can be placed on their exchanges. Obvious examples include the buying of rounds of drinks in turn or the splitting of bills when friends go out together somewhere. What is noticeable in most such cases, though, is that equivalence is not calculated precisely on the basis of what each side consumes. Usually it is achieved by a more rough and ready calculation, which serves to indicate that each side is willing to give to the other, while nonetheless ensuring that neither is in the other's debt. Indeed, on occasion, perhaps especially where the friendship is not totally secure or where there is some imbalance of resources, each side may almost rival the other in trying to make sure that it pays its full share, so as to ensure that no advantage is taken. In this, friendships are clearly the opposite of traditional market relationships. Similar processes are involved when the exchanges do not entail such an explicit financial value. For example, other things being equal, friends often tend to alternate visits to one another's house, especially for invited occasions like dinner parties or card-playing evenings. Statements like 'We really must have the 'Xs' back for a meal soon' or 'We owe the 'Ys' an invitation' are indicative of the mental – and sometimes literal – accounts kept, and reflect the desire to keep the transactions within the friendships in some sort of balance. The occasional giving of gifts within friendship serves much the same ends, especially, for instance, taking wine, flowers or chocolates when going for a meal at a friend's house or going to stay with them for a longer period.

Friendship involves more than these forms of sociable exchange, however. Friends also help each other out in various ways and perform different tasks for one another as needed. While such services are given because of the fact of friendship, there is, nonetheless, a mild pressure within these relationships to ensure that there is some sort of balance maintained. Certainly, people often worry about whether it is appropriate to ask friends for particular help or favours unless the help is part of a continuing exchange or they have some obvious way of repaying the friend. Normally they are wary of making demands that the other may find imposing and are probably more sensitive of the possible cost to the friend than is the friend him or herself. The friend, indeed, may be quite happy to oblige so that, at some later though unspecified time, he or she can in turn call on the other when some equivalent form of help is needed. In the end though, if the calls for help and the demands made become too heavy and are not reciprocated, then the friendship may well break down, either abruptly or through a gradual process as the feeling grows that the friendship is just being used (Wiseman, 1986; Willmott, 1987). Usually this state of affairs does not arise, however, as where there is a unilateral need for assistance it is the friend in need who backs off and refuses assistance, even when it is offered, so as not to become too indebted. (Some of these issues will be considered more fully in Chapters 6 and 7.)

A balance also tends to be maintained within friendship in terms of the emotional investment that each side commits to the tie. Certainly, as writers like Suttles (1970) have suggested, one important aspect of friendship is the gradual unveiling of private information about the self that is not for general consumption. Normally this process proceeds in tandem, with each friend revealing a more or less equivalent amount to the other. Unless there is good reason, like a precipitous personal crisis in the life of one of the friends, any consistent imbalance is likely to threaten the friendship. Either one side will feel the other is not showing sufficient trust or, therefore, commitment to the friendship, or the other will feel that more is being demanded of the relationship than he or she is willing to give. The result in either case is likely to be that the friends drift apart.

In such ways as these the balance of exchange within friendships tends to be maintained. Each side is able to ensure that he or she is neither abusing the friend, nor being used. The problem here, of course, is that ideally friendship is not concerned with such matters. The friends are friends, not for what they give or receive, but because they like each other and have developed their relationship accordingly. Explicitly calculating a cost-benefit analysis of the friendship is, indeed, an indication that the relationship is less than friendship, as friends are not really supposed to worry about such matters. In part, the way this contradiction is handled is by both sides monitoring themselves to ensure that whatever is received is in some appropriate way reciprocated. But in addition, the spirit of friendship is adhered to by keeping the transactional equivalence implicit, rather than making it explicit. In Naegale's (1958) terms friendship is characterised by an 'infrequent reciprocity' so that 'repayment' is not necessary immediately, but only after some period of time has elapsed. This camouflages the centrality of exchange to the relationship, demonstrates both the trust and apparent altruism of the friends and, of course, ensures the continuation of the tie through a time-lagged series of reciprocated transactions.

Equality, then, can be recognised as an important structural characteristic of friendship. Friends regard and treat each other as equals and sustain a long-run equivalence in their transactions. Given this structural property of the relationship, it is not at all surprising that the majority of friendships occur between people who occupy broadly similar social positions. There is, of course, nothing within the notion of friendship itself that requires this to be so, but the economic and social divisions within the society certainly encourage it. In other words, friends are normally of roughly the same age and class position. They also tend to share similar domestic circumstances, to be of the same gender, to have similar ethnic backgrounds and, where it is of social consequence, to belong to the same religion (Lazarsfeld and Merton, 1954; Hess, 1972; Fischer, 1982). A number of reasons exist for the broadly equivalent structural location of most friends. Most obviously, because of the way social and economic divisions pervade every aspect of life, people who share similar backgrounds and current experiences are most likely to meet each other and thus have the opportunity to become friends. Given the organisation of social life, the chances of people who occupy significantly different positions in the social structure encountering each other in contexts that encourage the formation of friendships are much smaller. Moreover, those who share similar social characteristics are likely to have much more in common than those who do not. Their orientation to life, their experiences and interests, their hopes and expectations for the future, their values and beliefs, the frustrations and problems they face, etc. are that much more likely to be compatible and thus provide a firm grounding for the development of friendship (Rosow, 1970; Hess, 1972; Jackson, 1977). Issues of status are also pertinent here, as the circle of friends and other associates which people maintain is one of the factors commonly used to locate them within the status hierarchy. Because birds of a feather are thought to flock together, there is some pressure to protect one's status by having as friends mainly people who are in a structurally similar position to oneself.

Factors like these are clearly important in explaining why friendship so frequently occurs between people with broadly similar social and economic characteristics. However, the equality which was identified above as a structural feature of friendship also plays quite a large part here. Clearly, it is much easier to treat as equal those who in fact are equal: who have the same economic resources, the same sorts of domestic commitment, the same status in the wider society, and so on. The necessary equality of the friends is harder to manage when contradicted by the criteria usually used to judge these things. (Coenen-Huther's (1987) insightful analysis of the importance of irony and joking behaviour in friendships where there are differences in status or values illustrates this point nicely.)

Although the ideology of friendship discourages it from being seen in this way, the crucial issue here is the resources that the friends can bring to the relationship. To begin with, friendship depends to some measure on the friends wanting and being able to engage in the same sorts of activity as each other. This is more readily achieved when their other commitments and obligations are similar, for otherwise finding the time and opportunity to service the relationship can become problematic. Equally though, being sociable and servicing friendships normally requires some financial expenditure. This may involve relatively small sums or much larger ones, depending in part on the financial position of those involved. The point here is simply that maintaining equivalence in the exchanges of the friendship is more difficult if the resources available to the friends for such purposes are unequal. When this happens the friendship is likely to atrophy. Importantly, these processes are effective, not just during the formative phases of friendship, but also later on. When the commitments and/or resources of one of the friends alter for some reason – for example, on marriage or divorce, or through a change in job – it is quite likely that the friendship will fade as it becomes difficult to maintain the balance of the relationship. These issues will be returned to again in Chapter 7.

FRIENDS AND MATES

These, then, are some of the implicit principles around which friendship is normally organised. In most respects, they apply most firmly to more rather than less close friendships, though, interestingly, a greater urgency may be felt about reciprocating exchanges and 'repaying' debts in friendships which are less secure than in those where a high level of mutual commitment is established. In these latter, asymmetrical exchanges can be more readily tolerated because of the high level of trust that exists between the friends (Roberto and Scott, 1986).

But while these principles govern friendship in general, their application is in practice nowhere near as neat as the above might imply. Obviously, they are not rules in the same sense as, say, the rules governing different games and sports. They are less rigid and less mechanical than these. So, while many friendships will accord well with these principles, some other ties will not, or at least not very fully. Yet these other relationships should not be ignored in analysing friendship patterns, especially where the concern is with the nature of informal sociability in general, rather than with friendship as an idealised form. The main point to emphasise here is that friendship is a social and cultural construction, rather than a 'natural' or inevitable way of ordering ties of informal solidarity. In consequence, as Cohen and Rajkowski (1982) recognise, there can be significant sub-cultural variations, not only in the percepts of friendship which people hold, but, more important, in the manner in which ties of sociability are routinely fashioned. Often these variations are reflected in the language that is used to characterise informal relationships. Certainly, it is noticeable that some sections of the population claim to have fewer friends than others. In particular many writers have suggested that the working class, loosely defined, has fewer friends than the middle class, even when they are more fully embedded in local neighbourhood and other social networks (Allan, 1979; Willmott, 1987). Often, though, these people use terms other than 'friend' to describe the informal relationships which they do sustain, 'mate' being the most commonly used, especially by males. (In the United States, the term 'buddy' is more frequently used, though, interestingly, its cultural connotations and social organisation appears remarkably similar to that of mateship (Rosecrance, 1986).) The clear implication here is that the way these relationships are organised marks them off as significantly different from friendships, thereby making the designation 'friend' seem somewhat inappropriate.

Because it illustrates the diversity there can be in the construction of sociability, the social patterning of mateship warrants fuller analysis. There is no intention here of stereotyping mateships, any more than the previous section was meant to imply that all those ties recognised as friendships are organised in a singular fashion. On the contrary, the main aim is to emphasise the variation that exists in the organisation of sociable relationships and indicate the problems inherent in an exclusive concern with a narrowly defined conception of friendship.

Clearly, mateship is a form of relationship which has much in common with friendship. It is, for example, a sociable relationship entered into voluntarily by people who are treating each other as equal. Yet it also differs from friendship in a number of respects. The most important difference between these two forms of sociability lies in the role that particular social contexts play in framing them. As discussed above, friendship is usually perceived to be a relationship in which context is relatively unimportant. Even if the friends routinely meet in one particular setting, this does not define the limits of their friendship nor account for its continuation. The context serves as a means of expressing the solidarity that there is, rather than being the rationale for the relationship. In theory, at least, though in practice it often does not work out this way, the relationship would continue in some form, even if the friends could no longer interact in the setting(s) where they currently do.

With mateship, on the other hand, social context plays a much larger part. In a real sense, the context actually defines the relationship and encompasses its boundaries (Allan, 1979). The relationship is seen more by those involved as existing principally because they happen to act together within some more or less narrowly defined social context. Whether it be work, a club of some form, a bar or whatever, this context does not just serve as a convenient forum for their meetings, but provides the recognised basis of the tie. Usually those who define themselves as mates – as distinct from friends – do not meet in other contexts except by chance. (And if they do, they may, like some of Rosecrance's (1986) informants, find the interaction difficult to sustain outside its normal setting.) In other words, despite the compatibility there is between them, they do not seek to develop the relationship they have by extending its field of relevance through involving each other in other aspects of their lives. This, of course, is the way in which most friendships are normally developed, as it expresses the purposeful-ness of the relationship and the commitment of those who are friends to their tie.

Because mateships are limited to particular social contexts, the boundaries of the tie are established more succinctly than is the case with friendships which tend to be more wide-ranging. In other words, this form of sociable relationship allows those involved to have a greater control of the 'content' of their tie, as it is focused more explicit on the setting in which they meet. Other aspects of their lives may be discussed and with time they may certainly get to know a great deal about one another, yet because they are not usually involved directly in these other aspects their access to such knowledge is more easily controlled. In particular, restricting relationships to specific contexts means that what goes on in the private domestic sphere of the home can be more readily concealed. To refer again to Bates's analogy, the 'rooms' of the self that the other is allowed to see are more clearly demarcated when the relationship is defined in terms of a given social context, rather than broadened into a commitment in which an a-contextual compatibility is highlighted.

There are other differences between mateship and friendship which stem from the different emphasis placed on context. First, mateships are potentially more fragile than friendships, for while the definition of friendship encourages the continuation of the tie, despite any change in the circumstances of the friends, mateships are, as it were by definition, liable to end when one or other, for whatever reason, no longer participates in the context which defines the relationship.

Secondly, while groups of friends often meet together, to be identified specifically as a friend usually implies some form of dyadic commitment. This is not the case to anything like the same degree with mates. Quite frequently, mates meet as groups in a way that, in effect, limits the specialness of any of the individual ties. In other words, mates are in a sense replaceable to an extent that friends are not supposed to be. If one person does not happen to turn up as usual it does not matter that much, for others will be there. This is not to say that some mates within the particular contexts will not be more important to the individual than others, but merely to emphasise that the overt rationale for interaction with mates is participation within the given setting, rather than interaction with a specific person, though of course each influences the other.

Thirdly, because of the contextual specificity of mateship, this form of relationship enables structural disparities between those involved to be ignored more readily than in friendships, as the boundaries provided by the context make them less relevant. As Oxley (1974) argues, equality within the setting can be maintained despite inequalities outside it in a way that would be extremely difficult in a relationship which was not circumscribed so tightly.

DISCUSSION

In some respects mateship appears to be an inferior or, at best, preliminary form of friendship. In other words, all of us maintain sociable relationships with others that we might hesitate to label friendships because they are characterised more by the above than by the criteria of friendship. They are ties that involve a level of friendliness, but which are not friendships as such (Kurth, 1970). However, as mentioned above, there is a good deal of research suggesting that the type of relationship described here as mateship is quite a typical way of organising sociable relationships amongst some sectors of the population, particularly working-class males. Whatever the reasons for this variation – and it would seem that restricting others' claims on limited resources plays some part – the point is that this way of organising sociable relationships is built into the routine of social life, as will be developed in Chapter 8. To this extent mateship can be seen as representing an alternative form of sociability and friendship, rather than just being a weaker or embryonic version.

It follows from this that the very concept of friendship is problematic in terms of analysing patterns of informal relationships. In essence, there are two problems that need to be recognised here, problems which at one level seem contradictory. First, the concept of friend is imprecise and socially variable. It is used in different ways in different contexts. It can cover virtually the whole gamut of relationship, from acquaintance to intimate, depending on the level of specificity called for in the given circumstances in which it is being used. In practice in social inquiry, when asked about friendships most people tend to assume a quite specific, relatively limiting notion of friendship. This tendency is, of course, encouraged further when researchers, in seeking a degree of precision, ask specifically about best friends or friends to whom the respondent feels closest. This relates to the second problem. While the concept of friendship is a flexible one, the more it becomes a topic of inquiry and an issue for reflection, then the more it approximates to a narrow cultural form. The consequence of this is that relationships organised along somewhat different lines – like mateships as discussed above – tend to be excluded from the analysis as apparently unimportant or, at least, of less significance and interest than 'real' friendship.

In consequence, the sociological study of friendship must look wider than solely at those relationships which people specify as friendships in response to a researcher's inquiries. While the use of the notion is revealing of the way in which people evaluate the informal relationships to which they are party, restricting the analysis to relationships categorised as friendships results in a rather biased perception of the actual involvement of individuals in ties of sociability. In the end, of course, the issue depends on why friendship is being studied in the first place. For most sociological purposes, though, where the aim is, broadly speaking, to comprehend the role of informal ties in social life, it is necessary to examine the full range of relationships of an informal type which individuals maintain. Questions can then be asked about these different relationships without assuming that a sub-set of this total – specifically acknowledged friendships – is necessarily of dominant interest. Though definitional problems clearly remain, from a sociological angle the focus must be with the pattern of informal sociability generally, which will include, though not exclusively, those relationships labelled as friendships. In this way it is possible to make some judgement about the role of friendship in social life. The categorisations people use remain important, but do not shut off lines of inquiry.

In arguing this way, no suggestion is being made that all relationships are equally important to the individuals involved. Clearly some are more central in people's lives and some more peripheral. The point is just that the particular label used to characterise a relationship is not of itself necessarily indicative of its importance. Instead, the analysis of friendship needs to start from a broader perspective and ask questions about the extent to which people are socially integrated. More narrowly, the focus should be concerned with what might be termed, without too much definitional worry, leisure-style relationships, i.e. informal ties which seem to the individual to be more, rather than less, voluntary. Questions can then be posed about the way in which the more significant of these relationships are constructed and organised, and, indeed, about whether they are transformed into more free-floating, individual relationships which are recognised as friendships.

What is evident from this is that a distinction needs to be drawn between subjective perceptions of informal relationships, on the one hand, and sociological analysis, on the other. For the latter purposes, the level of intimacy and strength of relationships, their organisational form, the participant's categorisation of them, etc., need to be complemented by an examination of the way that the various different informal ties which the individual maintains fit into the pattern of his or her life. The different use made of various ties, the calls that can be made on them, the boundaries that are established around them, the extent to which they are incorporated into, or insulated from, other aspects of the individual's social being, are all important for understanding the nature of friendship, generically interpreted, in everyday life. Certainly, it is wrong to assume that the significance of informal sociability and ties of friendship in general can be understood adequately by focusing principally on 'close' friendships. There is more to friendship than such approaches allow, common though they are.

3

FRIENDSHIP, CHOICE AND CONSTRAINT

In Chapter 2 the argument was made that friendship is not just a matter of volition and personal selection. Certainly, friendship is characterised more by these factors than other forms of relationship are, but nonetheless the opportunities to form friendships and to become socially involved with others are patterned and shaped by a range of external constraints. What friends do with one another, how they spend time together, how often they meet, the very character of their relationship, are also affected by factors over which the individual may have little control. This chapter will be concerned with examining how friendship patterns are constrained in these ways and with showing how structural factors, in addition to issues to do with personality and volition, need consideration in analysing friendship.

A major difficulty with much of the previous literature on friendship is that it rather isolates particular friend relations. It tends to look at the characteristics of ties individually, but fails to conceptualise them collectively in a way that highlights their social patterning or encourages a more structural perspective. Traditional approaches concerned with relating an individual's ties of informal solidarity with wider social factors drew on the notion of 'community'. Fuelled by the long-standing debate over the impact of urbanisation on patterns of social integration, the common paradigm involved contrasting social life in contemporary urban areas with the solidarity found in 'traditional' rural communities. Yet, while the concept of community appeared to provide a model for linking an individual's behaviour and relationships to the structure of his or her environment, the ambiguities and contradictions implicit in the concept limited its sociological utility. As a variety of writers have argued, defining the concept adequately has proved extremely difficult (Bell and Newby, 1971; Fischer *et al.*, 1977). This is partly because of the problems of overcoming its geographical implications, which are of little consequence in an age where rapid transportation is available to many, but mainly because community as a concept carries with it a good deal of 'normative baggage' about the way in which social life should be organised. The prescriptive elements built into our understanding of 'community' over the years render it of little use for analysis or even for description.

One of the more interesting attempts to overcome the inherent geographical and ideological biases of 'community' perspectives was formulated some thirty years ago by Elizabeth Bott in her study of marital roles (1957; 1971). Recognising that few urban localities operate as cohesive systems, Bott argued that people's actions should be understood in the context of their 'immediate social environments', that is, 'the network of actual social relationships they maintain' (Bott, 1971, p.99). In my view, this concept is particularly evocative and suggestive as a format for connecting the individual and the social, the personal and the structural. As such, it is most helpful for facilitating thinking about the way in which friendship patterns are constrained.

As is well known, Bott proceeded to analyse the social networks of her respondents, arguing that the structure of the personal relationships maintained by them and by their acquaintances was correlated with the organisation of their domestic life. In essence, her thesis was that the more close-knit or dense a couple's social network, the more segregated their roles within marriage were likely to be. This thesis has received a good deal of critical attention from sociologists over the years, not just because it helped to provide a way of understanding the social factors that shape marital roles, but also because it was the first example of the rigorous use of network analysis within sociology. While many disagreed with aspects of her substantive argument (e.g. Fallding, 1961; Platt, 1969; Harris, 1969; Toomey, 1971), most accepted that, along with another anthropologist John Barnes, (1954), she had opened up a new style of analysis that promised to overcome the well-recognised problems associated with 'community' approaches.

Since then, the whole area of social network analysis has opened up, generating much research effort, numerous symposia and, indeed, a specialist journal, *Social Networks*. In the process, use has been made of increasingly sophisticated mathematical modelling so as to be able to specify more precisely the social consequences of the sets of personal relationships that individuals maintain. However, it is questionable whether these developments within network analysis have actually resulted in the sociological advances they initially seemed to promise, at least in the area of family and community studies. Much use is now made of the language of network in them, but relatively few studies incorporate anything approaching a rigorous analysis of network structure into their argument in the way that Bott did. No doubt this is partly because of the methodological difficulties entailed in collecting full information about the structure of social networks. While it is relatively straightforward to collect data on an individual's relationships with his or her associates, ascertaining the strength and nature of any ties that exist between these other people is more complex. In addition, though, there are questions that need to be asked about the utility of network analysis as such for understanding the nature of informal ties.

In particular, the translation of 'immediate social environment' into 'social network' may render the former concept less interesting and less useful for analysing informal relations than it really is. What matters from the viewpoint of sociology is how an individual's life is constrained and structured by social arrangements and patterns of organisation over which he or she has limited control. With friendship, the issue is how freedom of choice is circumscribed, how apparently voluntary action is bounded and less free than it appears. Now, in many ways the idea of social network seems to be the embodiment of such an approach because the constructed network itself has an analysable structure that in theory, at least, can be related to patterns of behaviour. This is the great attraction of the approach as exemplified in Bott's work. If marital behaviour is linked to network structure, then so too could many other aspects of social organisation be. Sophisticated new techniques for analysing network structure have been developed as a consequence.

Yet it can be argued that this concept of structure is, in fact, a very limited one, and one which in a sense is distinctly unsociological. In particular, considering an individual's immediate social environment to consist simply and solely of the configuration of personal relationships he or she maintains — leaving aside any questioning of the operational procedures and equivalences involved in characterising a relationship as a link in the constructed network (see Allan, 1979) — is in essence a very individualistic approach. It fails to incorporate into the analysis of informal relationships anything wider than the informal relationships themselves. They, or at least their patterning, become their own explanation. In consequence, the network approach can give only a partial answer to the sorts of question which should be central to a sociology of friendship, such as, 'How come relationships are generated and maintained in the forms they are with the various different people an individual meets?' and 'What is it that structures and shapes the possibility of the network being as it is in the first place?'.

The beauty of Bott's concept of immediate social environment, as exemplified in the work of Lockwood (1966) and his followers, as well as by Bott in her discussion of class experience, is that it conjures up a vision broader than this. It is a conception which highlights the interplay between the individual, whose environment it is, and the social structure as it is lived and experienced by that individual. In other words, it offers a form of mediation between the social and the personal. But it does so only if social relationships are considered in a full sense, rather than simply as personal ties. The point here is the simple one that each individual is affected by social relationships – such as those based on gender, class, occupation and geography – which operate at a level above that of the individual. They are genuinely structural, rather than personal or individual, yet they have an impact on the individual which varies depending on their overall constellation. This constellation forms an individual's immediate social environment against which his or her actions need to be interpreted. In a nutshell, what is being suggested is that if we take the concept of immediate social environment seriously and recognise that an individual's personal relationships cannot be explained solely in their own terms, nor through a simple exercise of choice, then we are led to focus on the broader social relationships that encourage or discourage, facilitate or hinder different patterns of personal relationship – and this does not just mean different networks in the limited, conventional sense – from emerging.

This entails more than simply correlating friendship patterns with class or gender or some other structural variable in a mechanical fashion. It is not sufficient just to examine, say, middle-class versus working-class patterns, nor even just to show how an individual's material circumstances influence friendship, for class, however adequately conceptualised, is by no means the only structural feature shaping the options open to people. Again, the advantage of 'immediate social environment' as a concept is that it recognises this. The 'environment' referred to is not one based on economic factors alone, but one formed by the full set of relationships impinging on an individual. Analytically these need separating, but not in a fashion that isolates their impact. It is the constellation of social relationships into which an individual is bound that matters. Unfortunately, in much of the literature on friendship, notions like class, age and gender are treated simply as traits that a person has in some form, rather than being regarded as features of the social landscape that facilitate or discourage to differing degrees, in interaction with other aspects of social topography, the emergence of particular social patterns.

So instead of translating 'immediate social environment' into 'social network', a broader conceptualisation is needed. With this in mind, it is useful to draw on recent leisure research and equate 'immediate social environment' with the notion of 'personal space' (Deem, 1982). As in leisure studies, the idea of personal space is intended to convey an image of a bounded area of relative freedom within people's lives. Patterning the boundaries of this space are the demands and restrictions placed on the individual by his or her position within the social structure and the roles and relationships this entails. The space that remains within the boundaries represents the opportunities he or she has to develop aspects of personal life in ways he or she chooses.

At issue in linking friendship patterns with personal space is the notion that some individuals have more space than others to develop and service informal relations, and that the space available to them is determined by the interaction of a range of factors which affect the boundary, rather than being the direct consequence of any one. As Hess (1972) develops, the number and nature of the friendships open to an individual depend on the total cluster of roles in which that person is involved. In other words, in the terms being used here, the personal space individuals have will affect not just the opportunities they have to meet with others and initiate friendships. It will also colour the character or content of their sociable relationships – the kinds of activity undertaken, the frequency of interaction, the degree of involvement, and so on. Though these are often perceived as matters of individual choice, the choices that individuals make are made within a context shaped by broader structural considerations (Jackson, Fischer and Jones, 1977; Wellman, 1985).

FACTORS AFFECTING PERSONAL SPACE

Class position

As indicated above, numerous factors affect the personal space that is available to people to organise friendships and other sociable ties. Amongst the most important are the individual's position within the division of labour and the material and economic circumstances that go with this (as well, of course, as the equivalent situation of those with whom he or she forms friendships). As Wellman (1985) shows most clearly, the nature of people's friendship circles is patterned in various ways by the social and economic relationships in which their work, whether paid or unpaid, involves them. The characteristics of their work, and their role within the division of labour more generally, will, for example, have an impact on their level of social integration, on the opportunities they have for forming friendships, and on the resources of money, time and, indeed, energy they have for sociability.

At a basic level, an individual's income, and indeed that of the household as a unit, is likely to be of some consequence. Obviously, what friends do with each other will depend in large measure on their common interests, but what those interests are and how often they are engaged in will also be influenced by the financial resources they have available. While it is possible for friends to do things together without spending much money, many forms of sociable activity require some level of expenditure. Even what appear to be relatively mundane things, like going for a drink with friends or playing sport, may in practice be limited by financial considerations.

However, given that sociability has a relatively low priority within most households' scheme of things, what matters most here is the access that people have to financial resources once the other obligations of the household, e.g. for mortgage or rent, food, heating, etc., have been paid. It is important to note that any resulting 'excess' will not be equally available to all household members, nor indeed need there be agreement over what counts as excess or over the spending that is given priority within the household. Numerous studies have shown that within many marriages husbands have greater control of resources and have more access to money for social expenditure than their wives (Hunt, 1978; Edgell, 1980; Porter, 1983; Pahl, 1983; Allan, 1985). This is particularly likely to be the case where husbands are the sole income earners within the household. But even when they are not, the dominant domestic ideology, with its emphasis on men as income earners and wives as household servicers, encourages the view that men have a greater right to spend time and money on leisure and a greater need to recuperate from the demands of their labour. As a consequence of this conventional division of resources within households, husbands frequently acquire more space for sociable activities than their wives.

Another important element related to an individual's class position is the actual work that the person is involved in and the way in which its organisation patterns his or her sociable ties, both inside and outside the workplace. Different shift patterns, different travelling requirements, different levels of physical and mental exertion will influence the extent to which individuals are willing and able to engage sociably with others once they stop work. Along with domestic commitments, the patterning of the demands that work makes on their daily routines will affect the time they have available for interaction with friends, the effort they are prepared to make and, consequently in some measure, the form that their friendships take.

Similarly, different types of work differ structurally in the amount of encouragement they provide for creating and sustaining relationships of a generally sociable form within the work context (Fine, 1986). Most forms of employment provide some possibilities for meeting with others and getting to know them. Generally those people working for large organisations are likely to share meal breaks and the like with fellow workers, and in most cases have some opportunity for informal interaction in the course of their work. Others who work in smaller-scale establishments will have fewer colleagues available, but may have more direct contact with clients or customers of one sort or another, some of whom may become well-known over time. Indeed, in some enterprises, especially in the professional service sector, it may be important for the well-being of the business that a range of sociable relationships is built up, as will be discussed in the next chapter. Clearly, the majority of workplace contacts do not develop into recognised friendships as such. Many remain just workplace ties, either through choice, convention (as with other mateships) or circumstance. In some cases, friendship may be impeded by competitive or hierarchical elements built into the work environment. Overall though, employment generally offers some possibilities for developing friendships, generically defined, though it is evident that the extent to which it does depends on its internal organisation.

Yet, while most forms of employment are socialised to a greater or lesser degree, there is one very important form of work which remains privatised. This, of course, is housework, which continues to be done by individuals working on their own. The organisation of this work provides relatively few opportunities of itself for sociable interaction. Because it requires little cooperation – as distinct from coordination – it is structurally isolating and does not provide much of a framework for developing relationships. On the other hand, the autonomy of the work – the relative freedom those involved have to organise their time within the limits imposed by the need to coordinate domestic schedules – allows some scope to develop and service the friendships they do have with others in a similar position. Of course, numerous factors intervene in this, including the domestic timetable itself, the organisational framework available locally for meeting others in the same situation, and class background. Plenty of research is now available demonstrating the isolation experienced by many full-time housewives, with those having fewest resources appearing to be the most disadvantaged (Oakley, 1974; Hobson, 1978; Allan, 1985).

Two other factors, related to people's material circumstances and which affect the character of their friendships, are worth discussing briefly here. First there is the issue of transport. Where friends have been geographically mobile, it is evident that access to a car will have some bearing on the ease and frequency with which they can meet. However, even in relatively local friendship networks, some form of transport is likely to be needed to maintain regular face-to-face contact with friends and associates. To put this the other way round, where people do not have effective transport, their day-to-day friendship networks will tend to be limited to the immediate neighbourhood. Similarly, the sorts of activity that they can engage in with friends are likely to be constrained in the absence of cars or other forms of convenient transport. Thus the availability of transport can have an important influence on the opportunities an individual has for developing and maintaining different types of friendship. However, access to private transport is linked to factors of class and gender. Though the gaps are closing, members of the middle class are more likely to have the use of a car than are members of the working class, especially those in low-paid work or dependent on state benefit, while in general men are both more likely to hold a driving licence and to have greater control of any car available to the household (*Social Trends*, 1983; 1987).

Secondly, it is worth mentioning again here the issues raised in Chapter 2 concerning the different cultural patterns taken as normal within particular socio-economic groups. These are likely to be related to the group's material conditions, but may, nonetheless, be seen as exerting an independent influence over the patterning of friendship. As discussed in the previous chapter, there is a tendency for members of different classes to organise their relationships on a different basis, with working-class males, especially, tending to have 'mates' rather than 'friends'. The use of the home to service friendships is an important element within this. Generally the middle class bring friends into their home and use it as a place for sociability. Many of the working class are much less inclined to do this, regarding the home as a more private arena normally reserved for 'family'. The extent to which this is so varies, of course, depending on the particular circumstances of those involved, probably being more typical of older, more stable working-class households than others (Williams, 1983 – see Chapter 8). The main point here is simply that such cultural conventions shape the nature and character of the friendships that people generate, patterning their development in different ways.

Gender

Like class, gender is a major structural influence on the personal space an individual has available for developing and servicing friendships. While differences in friendship patterns between the two genders will be discussed fully in Chapter 5, it is worth emphasising here that the opportunities that males and females have for friendship will differ because of their different positions within the wider social structure. The single most important factor in this is the responsibility that the great majority of women have for much of their lives for the domestic care of other household, and sometimes extra-household, members.

Earlier it was argued that full-time housewives are structurally isolated because of the absence of any opportunities built into their work which facilitate their meeting with others. To some degree women who combine paid employment with domestic work can overcome this isolation. However, as many studies have recently shown, the very act of combining paid and unpaid work can leave women with relatively little time free for other activities. Where this happens the space there is in their lives for friendship and sociability is likely to be constrained. Notwithstanding the difficulties there are in specifying 'free time', obviously some people do have more time available than others in which to service friendships. As with all leisure, what matters is not just the total amount of time that domestic and economic obligations and commitments require, but also the distribution of this time. By and large, the more 'bitty' and piecemeal the other demands made of one, the less easy it will be to find time to meet with others. One of the dominant characteristics of much women's work within the home is precisely that it is fragmented and 'bitty' (Oakley, 1974).

In addition, the value of 'free time' for creating and servicing friendships depends in some part on the contexts in which that free time can be spent. While this is clearly affected by the distribution of the time available, it is also patterned by the normative rules governing people's access to different sociable arenas. Here, too, there are important differences between males and females, for generally men have greater access than women to what can be loosely called non-domestic arenas of sociability. Much of public life is more open to men, not just because they are likely to have fewer domestic responsibilities to constrain their participation, but also because the leisure organisations and associations there are have been built up over time to cater more for their requirements than women's.

Moreover, these organisations continue to be controlled and dominated by men. Whether the focus is on formal organisations like political parties or trade unions, less formal associations like sporting clubs or other recreational and interest-based clubs, or on explicitly sociable facilities like pubs or social clubs, the majority are distinctly male-oriented. There are comparatively few such organisations which are specifically aimed at women, though the number is undoubtedly growing (Dixey and Talbot, 1982; Deem, 1986). Furthermore, those which are formally open to both genders often operate on informal principles which make them more readily accessible to men. Through various more or less subtle mechanisms, women are often made to feel uncomfortable or unwelcome, and, indeed, occasionally unsafe, unless they are accompanied by a male. (For a vivid account of how some of the less subtle of these control mechanisms operate, see Whitehead, 1976.)

While the number of leisure-oriented organisations open to women is certainly increasing, many of them are in a sense less sociable than many male-dominated ones. What is meant by this is that while the majority of male-dominated voluntary clubs and associations have a specific activity as their rationale – be it horticulture, bridge, a particular sport or whatever – most also have built into their organisation opportunities before and after, or even independently of, the activity for socialising. Clearly, the provision of a clubhouse or some other regular meeting place, preferably with bar facilities, is advantageous for this, though not essential. Organisations catering specifically for women are somewhat less likely to have the use of facilities like these, which provide an arena for socialising with other participants. This may, of course, change when and if leisure provision ceases to be so male-biased. However, the fragmented nature of the demands which domestic servicing consistently makes of many women renders this unlikely, as, to a lesser extent, do the social conventions surrounding women's unaccompanied public consumption of alcohol. Together with the other factors discussed here, the result is that the majority of women have less personal space than most men do for developing ties of sociability, though, of course, there will be wide variation in this, depending on the individual's other circumstances.

Domestic relationships

The patterning of an individual's existing personal relationships also affects the amount of space he or she has available for friendship. At first glance, this seems very similar to a concern for the effects of social network structure on the ties included within it. To some degree it is, but it also involves the extent to which the content of existing relationships encourages or discourages involvement of different sorts in other ties. What matters is the scope and opportunity these relationships allow for other forms of social participation to develop and for ties of friendship to be enacted in various ways. Clearly, the most influential set of relationships in these respects will be those which are most central to the individual. For the majority of people, this will be the domestic group itself, principally the tie of marriage and the constraint of children. However, other relationships will also have some influence over the sociable patterns that are maintained.

Consider the marriage tie. Marriage shapes the personal space available to an individual, not just through the explicit demands and cooperation of the spouse over issues like domestic labour or going out alone, but also because the quality of the marital relationship will open or close possibilities for social interaction (Hess, 1972). For example, to draw on Bott (1957) again, where spouses are firmly embedded in separate kin networks, it is likely their leisure patterns will also be separate. In all probability the development of friend and other informal ties will further reflect this division. If nothing else, the couple are likely to have agreed, implicitly or explicitly, that their home should not be used for socialising with non-kin, at least not while the other is present. Where, on the other hand, the couple normally expect to be involved together as a couple in leisure activities, this is less likely to be so, and each will offer the other possibilities for engaging in informal relationships and support for friendships.

However, it is not just the patterning of the marital tie that matters here. More generally, the space there is for friendship will be affected by the overall constellation of obligations and responsibilities that an individual has for other members of his or her family. In other words, personal space is influenced by a person's family role and the stage they are at in the family course (Wellman, 1985). In particular, those who have responsibility for dependants – young children and in some cases dependent elderly – are likely to find that the opportunities open to them for sociable ties are constrained by the level of care they have to provide. As already indicated, such constraints usually affect women more than men, but both genders are likely to find that domestic and familial responsibilities shape their 'sociable options'.

Of course, this does not necessarily mean that once people are free of such constraints they will inevitably become highly active sociably, for the patterns generated in earlier phases are likely to continue to have some impact. As an illustration, consider married women whose children are no longer dependent. For many such women, the independence of their children represents something of a shift in their structural location, certainly more than it does for most of their husbands. In particular, while they are likely to remain responsible for domestic servicing, the amount, nature and necessary scheduling of that servicing will alter as children mature and leave home, unless, of course, they are involved in providing care for an elderly parent. In turn, they are likely to find their employment less demanding as combining paid and unpaid work becomes that much easier to manage. As a consequence, women in this domestic position are more likely to be able to construct consolidated periods of time in their schedules to devote to sociability.

Yet the extent to which women can alter their patterns of friendship at this time will still be influenced by their previous experience. To begin with, as discussed above, the majority of friendships are developed and sustained within particular social contexts. While women with fewer domestic responsibilities are likely to have greater access to such contexts, their access is in general still more limited than men's. Class position also continues to be of consequence here, as middle-class women have been more able than their working-class counterparts to generate the necessary organisational infrastructure to encourage participation in new pastimes and ventures.

On top of these factors the organisation of the marriage will continue to exert its influence, for it is unlikely that patterns will alter radically just because a new family cycle position has been reached. Thus, in a marriage where sociability has tended to be segregated, a wife is likely to continue to have comparatively little opportunity to develop her own independent circle of friends, especially if her husband is relatively inactive, so that his presence in the home encourages it to be viewed as 'family space'. In such circumstances, a wife is likely to continue to direct her attention more towards her children and grandchildren. If, on the other hand, sociability has been more joint throughout the marriage, wives are likely both to have developed friendships through their husbands' social participation and to experience fewer problems in establishing appropriate contexts for servicing these ties. In all likelihood, these patterns will continue in the post-parental phase of the marriage, with wives having relatively wide friendship circles, in the main shared with their husbands. In turn, such wives are less likely to focus their attention so heavily on their children and grandchildren, though, of course, these relatives will still be of consequence in their lives.

Existing friendships

As well as domestic and familial relationships affecting the space there is for friendships, the existing pattern of friendships can also shape the extent and form of any new sociable ties. While it is obviously wrong to suggest that friendship circles can become full in any simple sense, there is in practice a limit to the number of friendships that can be actively sustained by most people. Certainly, some friendships may continue, despite very little contact or active involvement in the short term, but normally relatively few actually do. Rather, because the majority of friendships and other sociable ties gradually fade and dissipate over time, unless there is some level of continuing interaction, the number that can be maintained is, in effect, limited.

To express this in a different, and perhaps more accurate, manner, some people have little need for new friendships because the space they have for sociability is already 'filled' sufficiently by existing relationships. The resources they have for friendship – and sociability does require time and, to some extent, money – are, as it were, committed elsewhere. This, of course, does not mean that new friendships will not develop, for friendship circles are dynamic; friendships do change over time as once-active friendships fade and new ones take their place. But it does mean that those who are already quite fully committed sociably are likely to put less effort into initiating new friendships than those who are not.

To develop this further, there are some circumstances in which people find it relatively easy to generate new friendships and others where it is much harder. Take geographical mobility as an obvious situation in which people are likely to need to make new sociable contacts. The ease with which they will be able to do this will depend on the sort of factors mentioned above, together with the 'institutional' support they receive on moving. But it will also depend upon the circumstances of those others they meet in their new situation. These others may at one level be very welcoming, especially in the short run, yet not be too concerned about developing these new ties into particularly effective friendships because their social circles are, in practice, already sufficiently full.

In such cases the institutionalised support there is for integrating newcomers is an important variable. Some organisations which are characterised by high levels of continuing mobility among their personnel are likely to have developed strategies and mechanisms for incorporating newcomers relatively quickly. Good examples of this are the patterns generated by colleges and universities for integrating new students at the beginning of each academic year, and the way in which some sections of the armed forces organise welcoming committees and other integrative mechanisms for those recently arrived on the base. Such devices may not always lead to established friendships, nor, indeed, be as uncoercive and voluntary as they sometimes appear. They nonetheless provide those involved with a simple means of meeting others and developing new sociable ties. Those lacking such support often find these processes much more difficult. Existing friendships also have an impact on one another, of course. This, after all, is very much the premise upon which network analysis is based. Here it is not simply a case that some new friends may be made through ties with existing friends, but rather that relationships may be affected by some of the other loyalties and antagonisms that exist within the network. For example, some friendships will become more significant in people's lives precisely because those involved form something of a clique or closed network (Milardo, 1986). They will be seen together, as well as independently, and thereby reinforce the solidarity that exists, possibly at the relative expense of other ties which are not part of such a closed network and thus do not receive the same level of effective social support. Similarly, the activities that such friends engage in together are shaped, not just by their own choices, though clearly these are important, but also by the choices of others who are involved in the effective clique.

Similar processes can also operate in a more negative fashion. Where, for example, two members of an individual's network dislike one another, this can lead to one or both of the relationships he or she has with them being disrupted. A spouse, for instance, may discourage or even attempt to veto a particular friendship, or the individual may find it difficult to maintain separate friendships with two people who are in conflict with one another. As the experience of friends of divorcing couples quite often illustrates, it is sometimes impossible to avoid taking sides or stop their antagonism intruding into the separate friendships. In such ways, patterns of existing ties can push the individual towards some relationships and activities, while more or less subtly discouraging participation in others.

FRIENDSHIPS OVER TIME

While rather few longitudinal studies of friendship exist (Adams, 1987), it is clear from common experience that people's involvement in different sociable relationships is liable to alter over time. As has already been emphasised, ties of friendship are not static, but change and evolve, usually quite gradually, sometimes more abruptly. What friends do together, how often they meet, the information which they disclose to each other, and so on will vary as their relationship develops and becomes more or less active. So, too, some friendships come to an end, often when one side's social, economic or geographical circumstances alter significantly, though the pace at which this happens will vary, reflecting the commitment there is to the relationship at the time. In part, these processes follow from what was written above, as the space people have for friendship itself alters with the circumstances that pattern their life. Yet, even without any structural change, modification to the 'content' of different sociable relationships normally occurs, with some friendships waxing as others wane. There is, of course, nothing determined or inevitable about these processes, for mutual preference and choice play a large part in them. Some friendships will continue, despite major shifts in the friends' circumstances, yet others which, it would appear, could be maintained without much difficulty are allowed to dissipate and become relatively inactive.

Of particular interest are those friendships which do last over time, especially when the circumstances of the friends result in there not being very much interaction between them. Friendship, in other words, is not just about current sociability, but also involves an emotional dimension which can be expressed and sustained in ways that do not involve very much face-to-face contact. Most important, it is possible for someone currently to have very little 'personal space' for the development of friendship according to the criteria discussed above, yet have a relatively full circle of friends, established during previous periods and maintained despite the changed circumstances in which that person now finds himself or herself. In such a case, these friends may be seen very little, but the emotional commitment to them remains, possibly being sustained by indirect means such as telephone or letter. An extreme example of this is provided by Dorothy Jerrome. One of her respondents – a deaf and disabled women in her eighties – corresponded with a total of one hundred people, amongst whom were her best friends (1981, p.190).

Clearly, the existence of such friendship circles raises questions about the notion of an individual's immediate social environment shaping his or her patterns of friendship. In a sense the implication of such instances is that it is not just a person's current circumstances that need to be considered, but also the circumstances they have experienced in the past and the opportunities they have had to build up their circle of friends. Also relevant, of course, is the extent to which the individual and the others involved, have made a deliberate effort to maintain these relationships over time, despite their changed situation. The explanation of friendship patterns, therefore, requires some form of time dimension as well as a consideration of the immediate social environment currently encompassing the individual.

Two comments are worth making about this. First, friendship networks in which the majority of friends are seen only rarely appear far from common. As has been mentioned before, the majority of friendships need an active input if they are to continue. To some extent, letters or telephone calls represent such an input, but generally the number of friendships that any individual maintains over any significant period in such a way is quite limited. Most friendships need some more or less frequent level of face-to-face contact, though the extent to which this is so depends on the way in which the friendship has been organised in the past, as well as on the experiences that the friends have been through together. Those regarded – for whatever reason – as 'close' or 'best' friends are more likely to continue in some form when circumstances alter. In contrast, those relationships which are seen as being based more on mutual participation in some sociable activity than on the individuals' special commitment to one another are clearly going to be more fragile. Once the individual ceases to be party to that setting the relationship is likely to be eroded. As suggested in Chapter 2 this appears to be a standard way of organising sociability among some sections of the working class, so that their sociable relationships are less likely to be maintained when circumstances interrupt their established course.

The second comment to make here is that, while the idea of personal space cannot of itself account for the continuing existence of some friendships from previous periods, it nonetheless remains useful for understanding the way in which these and other more recent sociable ties are currently organised. In other words, what matters is not just the number of friends that an individual has from different periods of his or her life, but also the way in which these relationships are patterned – their 'content' and social organisation. Take the example from Jerrome's study, quoted on page 45, of someone whose current position is highly constrained, yet who, through letters, is able to keep in touch with a wide range of friends made in previous periods of her life. While the number of friendships she has managed to maintain is not strictly limited by her present situation, what is quite evident is that this has a radical effect on the nature of those ties and on the ways in which they are serviced. Thus, even under these circumstances the notions of 'immediate social environment' and 'personal space' remain useful for analysing the patterning that there is in friendship, though, clearly, biographical experience and the personal strategies developed for maintaining friendships are also important (Matthews, 1986).

CONCLUSION

In this chapter the argument that friendship and sociability need to be seen as socially patterned and constrained has been made quite strongly in an attempt to counter the claims implicit in much of the literature, and, indeed, in everyday notions, that friendship is just a matter of choice. As emphasised above, rather than being freely chosen, the patterns of friendship, in a generic sense, which individuals sustain, are shaped by the whole interactive complex of material and social constraints that impinge on them – what, at the beginning of the chapter, was termed their immediate social environment. The overall constellation of these structural factors affects not just the opportunities that individuals have for meeting other people sociably and forming friendships, but also the 'content' of the relationships in which they are involved – the sort of activities engaged in, the frequency of interaction, and in some instances the emotional depth of the relationship. Once raised, this point is quite obvious, but it is an issue which research into friendship has so far failed to develop.

Nonetheless, choice plays a larger part within friendship and sociability generally than it does within most social relationships. The structural opportunities there are for developing and servicing friendships certainly shape what is possible, but within this individuals have a good deal of control over how their friendships operate. This is precisely the significance of the term 'personal space', for, as stated above, it suggests a more or less bounded area within which the individual has a relatively high degree of autonomy. Even here, of course, individuals are not entirely free to develop their friendships as they choose, for the organisation of friendship is an interactive process. In principle, at least, each party to an actual or potential friendship is as free as the other to influence its path, and consequently the choices each can make are limited by the choices made by the other – each of which is, of course, patterned to some degree by their different immediate social environments in the ways outlined above.

4

FRIENDSHIP AND
SOCIAL ORGANISATION

As discussed in the introduction, the sociology of friendship has in a number of respects not been very sociological. The questions posed in much of the research that has been published have tended more towards the traditional concerns of social psychology than mainstream sociological interests. To quite a large extent this is because friendship has usually been taken as being essentially voluntary and non-institutionalised, as a matter of individual choice rather than social construction, and therefore somewhat peripheral to the principal concerns of sociology. While friendship has obvious personal significance for those involved, it appears not to be integrated into the mainstream of social and economic life in the way that, say, the family, employment or even religion are. The dominant research issues have consequently tended to focus on friendship as it affects the individual – how many friends an individual has, what attracts particular friends to one another, how different strategies or styles of friendship are related to personality or to biographical experience, and so on – but little attention has been paid to the significance of friendship at a social level. For example, there have been few studies which specifically analyse the social or economic use that people make of their friendships – how friendships are drawn on to further interests; the way they are used by people to cope with the various contingencies they face; the part that sociable relationships play in the daily routines that make up our lives, etc. It is questions like these that are the focus of this chapter. In essence, it seeks to examine the social significance of friendship by analysing the role it plays in social organisation.

As discussed in Chapter 2, in doing this it is important to adopt quite a catholic stance towards friendship and not restrict the analysis to those friendships which are recognised as being especially close. The tendency in much of the research literature to ask about 'best' or 'closest' friends not only leads to a rather biased view of friendship in general, as a result of at least some of these friendships being special precisely because they are different from more run-of-the-mill sociable ties. (In particular, they are often sustained despite physical separation and rather limited contact.) It also often results in the analysis of friendship being rather decontextualised and, in turn, idealised, so that questions about the social utility of friendships are rarely pursued in the same depth as matters like strength of feeling or frequency of contact are. The focus in this chapter is much more on the role of friendship within social life, and in order to analyse this adequately it is necessary to consider the range of friendships an individual maintains, however these may be characterised, within the framework of the social contexts in which they develop. By so doing it will be possible to locate friendship within a broader canvas than is normal and analyse its social significance more satisfactorily.

The different relationships within an individual's friendship circle or, as it is sometimes called, sociability network, will not, of course, all be equivalent. They will vary in terms of settings of interaction, the feelings of identity and closeness, the activities to be engaged in, etc. Each relationship within the network will be characterised by its own series of negotiated, though generally inarticulated, exchanges. These exchanges, which can be taken as defining a relationship and marking off the boundaries of what is and is not appropriate within it, will emerge through the interplay of diverse factors, including personal choice, the contexts of interaction and the routine conventions there are about the way in which such ties should be organised. However, the specific nature of these exchanges will also depend on the current situation and circumstances of those involved: the resources they have to devote to each relationship; their domestic commitments; their work demands, and so on. Such factors will shape the specific needs of those involved and consequently pattern the use they make of different friendships and the benefits they obtain from them.

With this as background, we can now turn to the main thrust of the chapter and ask about the role that friendship plays within the social fabric and attempt to assess its social significance. As will by now be clear, the focus will not be so much on the rights and obligations that friends have towards one another, as it might be in analysing more institutionalised relationships, but rather more on the sorts of assistance and service that in practice friends give to each other. The issue is what they see as relevant to their relationships, what they feel they can ask of different sociable relationships, and how these exchanges are related to wider issues of social organisation. In a sense the main premise of the chapter is that friendship is not just about liking people, emotional commitment or a sense of worth, important though these are. Friendship is also a resource that we use, to differing degrees, to get through the everyday contingencies of living, further our social and material interests and help sustain our social identity.

COMPANIONSHIP AND SOCIABILITY

The most obvious benefit of friendship is the sociability and companionship that friends provide. Whatever the particular form of relationship, being with friends, spending time with them, sharing activities and pastimes, discussing issues of common concern, and the like are valued for their own sake. Whether the focus is active or passive, whether it involves some special event or, as is more usually the case, doing nothing out of the ordinary, interaction with friends provides, amongst other things, a distraction from the more serious matters of life, a sense of involvement and participation in the social realm and a means of expressing one's character and individuality. In practice, most of us take the integrative features of sociable ties for granted and have little need to reflect on their importance to us (Wenger, 1984). But, as studies of the housebound elderly, mothers with young children and the unemployed have shown, their real significance becomes apparent when, for some reason, our opportunities for friendship and sociable interaction become restricted (Oakley, 1974; Hobson, 1978; Hunt, 1978; Warr, 1983; McKee and Bell, 1986).

It is useful to distinguish two aspects of sociability and friendship here: participation in social activities, on the one hand, and companionship and intimacy, on the other. Clearly, it is possible to participate socially with others in particular activities on a more or less routine basis without those others becoming intimates or even being recognised as friends. For example, it is possible to maintain sociable relationships with, say, neighbours, fellow members of a sports or social club, or people who are co-participants in an evening class, without engaging in any other activities with them or revealing much about one's self. Equally, it is possible for friendship to involve a good deal of intimacy without sharing many activities. As mentioned, this is the case with many close friendships where distance prohibits regular involvement. In other cases, too, friends may confide a good deal in one another, yet through circumstances, such as physical handicap, not actually do much else together. In the author's Seldon Hey research (Allan, 1979), a good example of this concerned Mrs. Baker, an elderly housebound woman, whose best friend visited regularly and provided a good deal of help, but where there was no wider interaction.

Most friendships lie somewhere in between these two forms, with various balances between activity and intimacy. Some, like the mateship form mentioned in Chapter 2, involve specific social activity outside the home and keep quite restrictive boundaries governing the matters considered relevant to them and the degree of intimacy permitted (Oxley, 1974; Allan, 1979). Others may make greater use of the home as an arena for interaction, a practice which generally encourages a degree of intimacy and self-revelation, though by no means inevitably so.

Yet, while there is a good deal of variation in the way that particular relationships within a sociability network are organised – and, indeed, systematic variation between the dominant forms within different networks, depending in part on the social circumstances of the individuals concerned – it is evident that companionship and sociability are not the preserve of any particular form of friendship. That is, whatever the 'rules' or 'boundaries' that are constructed for the various relationships in a sociable network, in their different ways they can all fulfil this integrative function to some degree for those involved. Thus, such factors as whether an individual interacts with the others involved in his or her home, at work, in a local club or social organisation, whether the person is seen individually, with his or her spouse or in larger groups, even whether the boundaries around the normal activities and topics of conversation are more or less tightly defined, are all relatively unimportant from this perspective. What matters here is that the relationships, to differing degrees, provide a forum for companionship and sociability that is socially rewarding and integrative.

FORMS OF SUPPORT

Besides providing sociability and companionship, friendships provide a good deal of personal support. Along with other primary relations, especially those with close kin, friends are a resource that is routinely used to handle whatever issues there are of concern in people's lives. This support can take a number of different forms. For analytical purposes these can be separated into moral and emotional support; practical assistance; and material aid, though in practice these distinctions are blurred.

Emotional and moral support

The range of emotional or moral support that friends provide clearly varies a good deal. However, simply talking over particular happenings and occurrences that are generating problems of a mild or more serious sort in people's lives, and discussing courses of action and response, is a routine feature of most friendships. The topics involved are normally quite mundane, though they obviously depend on the specific circumstances of the individuals concerned and the parameters they have constructed around their relationship. Thus, colleagues or workmates may discuss issues to do with their work performance or with the running of their organisation with one another. Adolescents may spend much of their time analysing their contacts and relationships with boy friends or girl friends. The practical problems of child care are likely to loom large in the conversations that parents of young children have with each other. Equally, other concerns may, in effect, be ruled out of court as topics to be discussed. Domestic problems may not be seen as legitimate matters to discuss with workmates; work-based difficulties may not be seen as relevant to friendships based more on, say, the neighbourhood or some common associational membership. The main point here is that moral and emotional support is not just provided by particularly close friends, nor only over matters of great personal moment. Rather, support of this sort is a common feature of most sociable relationships. All but the most perfunctory relationships involve discussion of issues of common concern and in this process function to provide the individual with moral support.

Of course, not all the problems we face in our lives are so mundane. Some are of major consequence, and concern matters which we regard as essentially private. Whether these be crises to do with marital problems, illness or death, family relationships, or whatever, we may well feel unable to discuss them with any but the closest friends who, we feel, know us particularly well and who can be relied on and trusted fully. Here the supportive role of the friend in providing advice and comfort is rather different from what is required in more mundane matters. Rather than being part of the routine exchange of issues and gossip, it normally involves a much more one-sided flow of support. As a result it requires a relatively high level of trust in the relationship, especially if the matter is thought to reflect discreditably on the self.

Interestingly, too, the process can work in reverse. That is, close friendships can develop between people who were previously not so close, as a consequence of one person's providing another with a high level of support at a time of need. Perhaps the most common circumstance for this to occur is when someone has previously experienced the specific problem now affecting the other. Thus, for example, someone whose marriage has broken up, whose spouse is dying of cancer or who is suffering domestic violence may find most support from someone in their network who has direct experience of these matters and find that a closer friendship is generated as a consequence. Indeed, in the case of domestic violence, the research literature suggests that many women are often too frightened or too ashamed to discuss their problems with any friends (or family) they may have. However, once the matter is in the open, they are able to establish quite strong friendships with others who have also been abused. An important factor operating in such cases is the balance that is maintained when both sides share what may be seen, however unjustifiably, as a stigmatising experience. (See Chapter 7.)

Practical support

As well as moral support, friends routinely provide help of a practical sort. They do such things as give each other lifts, pick up items of shopping, keep a check on the house when people are away, cover for one another at work, provide advice on topics on which they have particular expertise, tape records, get things cheaply if they have the appropriate contacts, look after children, help on domestic projects, and so on. In other words, people use their friends as resources to help cope with the more or less mundane demands made of them. While the degree to which they are drawn on will, in practice, vary quite widely depending on circumstances, friends are in this sense part of the means by which most of us manage our day-to-day affairs (Litwak, 1985; Willmott, 1987). The services and help they provide for one another are, as Wellman (1985, p. 169) emphasises, 'much more than symbolic expressions of friendship'. They represent 'a wide range of flexible, low monetary cost, trustworthy, and efficient resources for domestic and paid work'. Obviously, friends are not the only people that we use in this manner. As many studies have shown, primary kin – i.e. parents, siblings and adult children – also provide each other with practical support in a whole variety of different ways. (See Allan, 1979.) Some authors, such as Litwak and Szelenyi (1969), have argued that, as a result of their likely different geographical location, different types of primary group member are able to provide different forms of assistance to one another. So, for example, because they are on hand, neighbours can do things that friends or kin who live some distance away cannot. While proximity certainly has a bearing on the type of help that can be given, it is somewhat artificial to regard kin, friends and neighbours as discrete 'primary group structures'. Not only are the majority of friends, and indeed often enough kin, relatively local, but in any case those neighbours who are drawn on in the ways specified are quite likely to be friends, in the generic sense used in this chapter. The point here is that in reality the others whom an individual draws on to help handle the different contingencies and concerns that he or she faces cannot be categorised as neatly as Litwak and Szelenyi's model implies.

Nonetheless, the general theme that Eugene Litwak has been developing throughout his career is certainly relevant here. Initially Litwak was concerned with the operation of what he termed the 'modified extended family' (Litwak, 1960a; 1960b; 1965). Essentially he argued that rather than being rendered isolated or obsolete, this form of family has, with the rise of bureaucracies within contemporary industrial society, become particularly salient. In a nutshell, because of its flexibility, the modified extended family is capable of reacting particularistically and in piecemeal fashion to the problems and issues which confront individuals. In this way it can serve to complement the operation of more rigid bureaucratic organisations by, as it were, smoothing the individual's path through them.

While aspects of Litwak's thesis have been heavily criticised (Harris, 1969), he has continued to develop the important theme that informal relationships are not social luxuries, as they are sometimes portrayed, but are quite central in the organisation of social life (Litwak, 1985). For him, informal relationships fulfil a major function by acting as resources that enable the individual to meet and fit in with the demands made of him or her by the relatively inflexible bureaucracies which dominate much of life. Like kin, friends are used to help in different ways to meet the sometimes conflicting requirements different organisations make and to fit in with their schedules. This is not just at times of crisis, when suddenly unpredicted demands are made of one – though, of course, at such times the practical and moral support of friends can be invaluable – but also more routinely. Indeed, to extend Litwak's arguments a little, it is not only in response to contingencies generated by different forms of organisation that friends provide practical assistance. More generally, people often draw on their friends to help them fulfil their more informal role obligations and realise their personal projects. In essence, the point here is that because they are informal and flexible, ties of friendship play their part in sustaining social organisation by helping individuals to coordinate the various demands made of them and achieve the more or less mundane goals they set themselves.

Which particular individual/informal relationship is drawn on and used for a given problem is an emergent, contextual matter. In other words, who is turned to will depend on the nature of the issue at hand, the developed exchange basis of the relationship and each side's social situation. There are no absolute or fixed rules here. Each individual is surrounded by a larger or smaller network of others, all of whom have different characteristics, different talents and skills, different opportunities, as well as different relationships with the individual in question. He or she may turn to one person for one matter, but to someone else for another. The person we ask to borrow a piece of decorating equipment from is not necessarily the same person we use to collect the children from school, nor again the person who helps us to solve some problem at work.

Of course, this is not meant to imply that everyone has an inexhaustible supply of friends who are all called on equally for support. By and large, most people draw most regularly on a small number of closer friends, maybe only one or two. Equally most people are somewhat wary of 'using' or 'taking advantage' of their friends, as was discussed in Chapter 2. Consequently, a good deal of thought is often given to the appropriateness of asking friends for substantial assistance or accepting it when it is offered. Indeed, the more extensive and personal the help and support required the greater the tendency to use primary kin, especially parents or adult children if they are on hand, rather than any but the closest friends. Primary kin relationships tend to be defined as more enduring and, in a sense, more instrumental than the majority of friendships. They can be used unilaterally more readily than the latter.

In contrast, ordinary, run-of-the-mill friendships are neither defined as being about providing help in the way that family ties are, nor in the main is their basis so secure. So while we certainly draw on friendships in a variety of ways, the need to demonstrate equality and reciprocity within the relationship remains important. Aside from particularly close friendships, the consequence is that the help we are routinely willing to ask of friends tends to be quite limited and immediate. This makes repayment and the maintenance of the balance of equality within the relationship easier to handle, though, of course, the more close the friendship is regarded as being, the less concern there generally is about asking for help, as trust in the relationship is well established.

As simple illustrations of the sort of limitation usually placed on the help which friends give, consider two of the issues mentioned earlier: shopping and child care. Only under quite rare circumstances – for example, after an accident or if someone is incapacitated through illness – would friends be used to do the household shopping. Normally it is only legitimate to ask them to pick up one or two items, and then only if they happen to be going to an appropriate shop anyway. In other words, this sort of favour is usually undertaken only if it does not involve the friend making a special trip or otherwise being put out very much. Similarly, there are conventionally limits on the extent to which friends are used for child care. While it is possible that a friend may be used for systematic, long-term child minding on a reciprocal or paid basis, it is far more usual for friends to be called on for shorter, more piecemeal episodes. The friend used is likely to be someone with young children of his or her own, so that the favour can be returned. Indeed, in many cases informal arrangements are likely to develop whereby each friend provides the other with a flexible back-up child care service to cater for the more or less haphazard contingencies they face.

Banal though these examples are, they illustrate the way in which the help friends give to one another is usually quite limited. Indeed, this banality is, in a sense, central to the argument being made here. The nature of the solidarity and the principles underlying the majority of friendships mean that those involved generally draw on one another only for relatively minor assistance. Most friends are only used for mundane favours which do not require them to put themselves out a great deal and do not involve much expenditure.

Such favours can be readily reciprocated in kind and do not involve high levels of obligation. But this does not mean that the practical support which friends give one another is socially unimportant. As argued earlier, limited though it may be, such support, in whatever form it takes, often plays a part in helping us meet our objectives and cope with the demands others make of us.

Material aid

Only on relatively rare occasions do friends provide one another with direct financial support. They may lend each other small amounts to cover, say, the cost of a round of drinks or admission to some event if one of them is short of cash, but on the whole do not enter into more significant loans with one another. However, friends do provide other forms of material assistance and financial benefit. The scale of this varies widely, in part depending on the structural position of those involved. In most cases the financial value of the transactions is relatively low, as is the case with some of the forms of assistance mentioned above, e.g., providing sporadic help with child care or lending friends implements they would otherwise have to purchase. In some cases they may have greater financial value, as when friends stay with one another for holidays, rather than staying in hotels.

While the economic benefits derived from friends are in most cases quite minor and do not radically affect an individual's economic position, some have argued that under certain conditions the economic contribution made through friendships and other informal relationships may become much more crucial. In the late 1970s and early 1980s in particular, there were suggestions that high levels of unemployment might lead to the development of a form of 'black' economy in which work was obtained and paid for on an informal, *quid pro quo* basis. In part, at least, the argument was that in areas of high unemployment, people with particular skills would do work for their friends and contacts in exchange for other forms of work that their friends, with their own different skills, would do for them. What, according to this view, would develop was an almost non-monetary system of exchange which depended in quite large measure on the maintenance of extensive circles of friendship. While there is, in fact, little evidence that systems of exchange do develop in the way envisaged – not least because unemployment is socially isolating, as will be discussed more fully in Chapter 7 – what is interesting about these ideas, from the present perspective, is that, unlike many other analyses, they do at least recognise that friendship can have an economic component.

Although not directly concerned with friendship *per se*, a number of other types of study have also illustrated this point. For example, empirical studies of the unemployed have shown that friendships, though not necessarily close ones (Granovetter, 1973), are of major importance in providing job information. Thus, in their study of redundant steel workers, both Morris (1984) and R. M. Lee (1985) show how the structure of the networks in which people are embedded patterns the flow of information they receive about job opportunities. (Also see Harris, 1987.) Though there appear to have been few equivalent studies of employed groups, it seems quite likely that at least in some occupations friends provide an important source of job information and recruitment. Equally, many studies of the way élites operate are premised on the idea that useful information routinely flows between people who have close ties, be they of kinship or friendship, with one another. Certainly, studies of the City suggest that interests are often furthered through information on investment possibilities that friends provide.

Studies of some professional groups are also of interest here, in particular those that Watson (1964) characterises as 'burgesses'. These are generally self-employed professionals, like GPs, solicitors and dentists, who are tied to a specific locality because their careers depend on establishing and maintaining a practice, rather than progressing through an organisational hierarchy. Because their livelihood depends in some measure on their ability to attract clients, customers or patients, it is in their interests to establish their reputation and become well-integrated in their locality. One strategy for doing this is to establish as wide as sociable network as they can, particularly with others in the area who act as 'gatekeepers' (Pahl, 1975). Thus they are likely to find it beneficial to belong to a range of local social organisations and societies through which informal relationships can be nurtured. Although unlikely to be seen in this way, establishing friendships with others who are powerful within the local social system can operate directly or indirectly to further their professional interests. The same may be true of self-employed craftsmen, though there seems to be little research on this. At times, of course, the use of friends for business purposes can lead to difficulties, especially in the public sector. The Poulson case (see Chibnall and Saunders, 1977) provides a good illustration of this.

The injunction against policemen mixing with 'known criminals' is also of interest here.

IDENTITY AND STATUS

In addition to providing various forms of support which help sustain social organisation, friendship is also important for the sense of identity it provides. Because informal ties of friendship operate independently of the formal role positions we play – even if many develop from relationships initiated within these roles (Hess, 1972) – within them we are able to express ourselves more freely than we normally can in other more institutional contexts, where norms of behaviour are constrained by role obligations and demands. This is not to suggest that patterns of behaviour within friendship are in some sense 'norm free'. This is certainly not the case. When we are with friends, whether close or more distant, we follow a range of social conventions that govern appropriate behaviour (Suttles, 1970). Nonetheless, to the extent that friendship involves generating ties of solidarity based on compatibility and liking independent of instrumental considerations, then friendship permits a greater leeway in expressing one's identity than most other roles do.

The whole idea of expressing our true or real self is, of course, one fraught with difficulty. As Goffman's early work demonstrated, we rarely act without an awareness of the image we are portraying and a sense of how others are 'reading' this. This applies to our interaction with the range of friends we maintain, as it does to other areas of activity, though, of course, the image we are attempting to portray is likely to be different (Goffman, 1959). However, the 'self' that is revealed in our dealings with our friends is closer to our self definition than the 'self' we portray in other contexts. In Goffman's own terms, friends are permitted 'backstage' more than most, gaining a better view of how our performance is constructed, and hence a deeper insight into what we are 'really' like. Within this there are variations and gradations in the extent to which different friends are permitted 'backstage'. To use Bates's (1964) analogy once again, some see more 'rooms' of our self than others, depending on the strength of the relationship and the boundaries constructed around it.

While the manner in which the self is presented in friendship is important, the support and recognition given to identity by friends is sociologically of greater consequence. What is involved here is an interactive process whereby friends help to shape and mould our self-image and give credence to our identity (Rubin, 1985). Traditionally within sociology, this has been recognised most fully in studies of minority or deviant groupings where the support of others involved in the same activities, or sharing similar beliefs, can have a major impact. (See, for example, Barnhart, 1976; Seiden and Bart, 1976; Willis, 1977; Levy, 1981.) Yet it is not just for individuals with somewhat unusual or deviant social identities that friends play a significant role in identity formation and maintenance. Throughout social life, friends are important in reinforcing, moulding, and, on occasion, challenging each other's identities, no matter how conventional or esoteric their content.

The processes by which friends do this are numerous and subtle. One way is through the emotional and moral support they give, which was discussed earlier in the chapter. Equally though, they may do it through humour, ribbing and joking about any pretence that we may have to be what *they* think we are not. The use of humour is a powerful mechanism within informal relations for reinforcing the parameters of identity. Mainly though, friendship serves to furnish a sense of identity through the topics of conversation, the views of the world portrayed, the discussion and argument that ensue, and the other 'content' of the ties. As Rubin (1985) suggests, it is in such mundane ways – through their routine and unexceptional involvement with one another, through their everyday inquests into actions and stances they have taken, through their recounting of past events and planning of future happenings – that friends effectively influence and affirm each other's social identities.

One further aspect of friendship's role in cementing identity stems from the equality that lies at the heart of these relationships. In essence, spending time socialising with others in relationships which are culturally defined as both voluntary and equal leads to an identification with those others. Despite any difference in temperament or personality there might be between you, the fact you are friends is taken as indicative of similarity. In this light it is interesting to note what happens when people's status and social identity alter. As raised earlier, and discussed more fully in Chapter 7, often new friendships tend to develop, and old ones atrophy, as a consequence of major changes in people's lives. Earlier it was suggested that this stemmed from friendship's basis in equality. Also at work here, though, is the process of identification that friendship involves. If a person's status alters significantly, this is likely to be reflected in his or her self-image and identity. Thus, to the extent the new status is relevant to the interactional basis of existing relationships, identification with these others is likely to be more problematic. Slowly these ties will be replaced by others which are more consonant with the new identity and which serve to bolster it more effectively. For instance, following Berger (1966), consider the case of someone who gains promotion, say to the rank of professor. Traditional role theory emphasises how the new incumbent will gradually pick up the accoutrements of the role and begin to behave like a professor. He or she may, for instance, modify the way they dress or the way they treat students, secretarial staff and junior colleagues. As part of the same process, though, it is also likely that the individual would gradually rid himself or herself of previous friends and associates and begin to spend more time in the company of other professors, and, as important, feel increasingly comfortable doing so.

In a similar vein, there are numerous accounts in the research literature of the way in which adolescent friendship patterns alter once courtship begins in earnest. From their being part of a same sex group or 'gang', the focus of their sociability shifts to other couples, which not infrequently results in previous, and as yet 'uncoupled', friends feeling somewhat betrayed (Willmott, 1966; Leonard, 1980; Griffin, 1985; Coffield, Borrill and Marshall, 1986). So, too, studies have shown how women returning to full-time education tend to lose contact with some of their previous friends – especially those who do not particularly value education – and develop ties with others more attuned and sympathetic to their new experiences (Levy, 1981; Suitor, 1987). While other transitions, in particular widowhood (Chapter 6) and divorce (Chapter 7), will be discussed later, these examples are sufficient to illustrate how friendship reflects status and cements social identity.

The social identification of friends has a broader significance. In studies of local stratification systems, patterns of sociability and friendship have frequently been used as a prime indicator of an individual's status position within a locality. In particular, the classic community studies of a generation or so ago frequently drew on such measures to assess where the boundaries of status could be drawn (Williams, 1956; Stacey, 1960; Littlejohn, 1963). Here the concern is with the level of social honour bestowed on individuals (and their families), which, interactionally, is revealed as much in patterns of social ease as patterns of deference. In this way, friendship relates to wider issues of status and stratification: whom you mix and associate with serves to locate you within a status hierarchy, in the process conveying images of character and social worth.

Of course, in small communities, ascertaining patterns of association and friendship and forming judgements about status is a relatively straightforward matter of observation. In larger communities, these patterns are nowhere near so evident, as only a small minority of the population living in them will ever be known. Furthermore, even where people are known, it is likely that one's knowledge of their friendship networks is partial, so that people cannot be 'placed' in such a ready manner. Furthermore, as Bell and Newby (1971), amongst others, point out, it is inappropriate to expect a single, unambiguous status system to exist within urban areas. Instead, what occurs is more a series of broad social levels entailing cross-cutting matrices of different social groupings (Stacey *et al.*, 1975). Nonetheless, the same general principle applies within such areas as in smaller communities: to the extent that they are known, a person's friends and sociable contacts are indicative of his or her social standing.

The argument here, then, is that informal ties of friendship help to sustain the individual's sense of self by treating him or her particularistically outside the given framework of more formal role behaviour. Within friendship, however strong or weak, it is the person who matters, not the positions that he or she holds. At the same time, however, the identity of the individual and the sense of self that person has is very much informed by the roles he or she occupies in other spheres of activity. In the vast majority of cases what goes on within friendship does not undermine formal role positions, but supports their meaning for the individual. There is, in other words, a form of articulation between these spheres (Hess, 1972). On the one hand, friendship provides a setting in which external role performance may be of little direct relevance, yet, on the other hand, many ties of friendship are built upon and reinforce the significance of these roles. At one and the same time friendship can serve to demonstrate the independence of the individual as a person from these roles while also giving recognition to their significance for the individual. At times, of course, activities within particular friendships may conflict with one's roles – on occasion, for example, there may be a clash between the demands of a spouse and those of friends, or, as in the cases mentioned earlier, providing favours for a friend may be seen as corrupt. In the great majority of friendships, however, there is no such tension. As Jerrome (1984) emphasises, friendship acts as a counterpoint to more formal role positions without threatening the performance of those roles. Dorothy Jerrome's study of a clique of middle-class, middle-aged women is worth discussing more fully, as it is, from a sociological viewpoint, one of the most valuable accounts of friendship produced in recent years. More than most writers she is specifically concerned with analysing how the socially integrative features of friendship operate, and within this context emphasises the way in which friendships can promote a sense of individual worth and distinctiveness, without in any way undermining social identities whose roots are located within the broader social formation.

The 'tremendous ten' was the name by which the group of eleven close women friends whom Jerrome studied referred to themselves. These women, who were all in their fifties or sixties, lived near to one another and frequently met with each other. They were all now relatively affluent, principally as a result of being married to men with successful careers. Though some of them were employed in some capacity, their main work had been that of supporting and servicing their husbands and families. Overall, they were capable, self-assured, lively women, proud of their achievements and content to enjoy all the material and social benefits their wealth and domestic circumstances now permitted. In particular, their affluence enabled them to lead relatively 'leisured' lives in which a good deal of time and effort was devoted to entertaining and socialising, activities which they all valued highly.

As evidenced by their giving themselves a name, this group of friends had a strong sense of group solidarity. This was also expressed in the rituals and ceremonies they had created for the regular, quasi-formal collective meetings they held in each other's houses. These meetings, together with their more everyday interactions, provided a forum where they were able to relax and enjoy themselves, away from any worries or concerns they may have had. Equally, though, they could confide in each other, discuss whatever issues were currently troubling them and receive advice and support. Through these friendships the women were able to express and validate their own uniqueness, worth and individuality. Their interaction with one another gave them a stage to get away from their other roles and responsibilities and a way of implicitly professing their self-identity.

Yet, as Jerrome shows so well, at the same time they were

reasserting, rather than countering or threatening, the dominant roles in which they were involved. Their emphasis on a particular form of feminity – that form which values appearance, looks, fashion consciousness, being a good hostess and entertaining well – clearly reflected and reaffirmed their position as wives/servicers of successful and affluent men. Similarly, while they might complain about their husbands' behaviour and discuss the state of their marriages, these comments were not a rejection of marriage or their role within it. The exclusion of husbands from the group allowed these women the freedom to be themselves, unencumbered by their marital roles. Yet, as Jerrome discusses, their exclusiveness and solidarity was in no way threatening to their domestic situation, instead providing moral support for it and upholding a conservative ideology of domestic life.

It is in ways like these that friendship can generally be seen to offer both an escape from more formal role positions and at the same time a reaffirmation of their significance. As Jerrome concludes, these ties act as 'the cement which binds together the bricks of social structure' (1984, p.715).

5

GENDER AND FRIENDSHIP

This chapter is concerned with the impact of gender on friendship. As Robert Bell (1981) suggests, gender is arguably the most significant of all social factors in shaping friendship patterns. Certainly, there is a cultural assumption that men's and women's friendships are different. Men tend to be thought of as having a greater propensity for friendship, to be more active socially and consequently, in general, to have somewhat larger friendship networks. Traditionally they are presented as having little difficulty in forming ties with others and as being better able to service and sustain them without petty squabbles or jealousies emerging. In contrast, according to the dominant stereotype, women's friendships are rather more tenuous. Not only are women seen as naturally involved more in domestic matters and less concerned with sociability outside the home, but the friendships they do have are often supposed to be less stable. There is quite a strong imagery of women being 'bitchy' about one another, gossiping and betraying confidences. Furthermore, many of the everyday concepts of sociability suggest friendship is more a male preserve than a female one. While 'friend' itself appears gender-neutral, many of the other terms used to describe sociable ties – such as 'mate', 'buddy', 'pal', 'mucker' – tend to have male connotations.

Of course, it is not only at an everyday level that images such as these receive support. Nearly all the great friendships from literature and history discussed in more philosophically oriented analyses are friendships between men. As elsewhere, women are curiously absent (Lewis, 1960; Sadler, 1970; Brain, 1976). Recently, too, the notion that men have a greater capacity for friendship than women has received explicit support from the work of socio-biologists like Tiger (1969) who suggest that gender differences in friendship patterns are innate. The argument advanced is that as a result of the dominance of hunting and gathering economies over the course of history, men's genetic inheritance came to have built into it a propensity for bonding with others which is absent in women. In brief, men's hunting role within such economies required the development of high levels of cooperation and trust between them, whereas women's role, being centred upon child care, was more individualistic. Over time, the argument goes, natural selection led to these characteristics becoming genetically embedded, so that men continue to have a greater inherent capacity for friendship and social solidarity outside the family.

Though few, if any, sociologists would support Tiger's genetic claims, they would accept that gender has a significant impact on the patterning and organisation of friendship. The purpose of this chapter is to examine the social processes which are at work in this. While the second part of the chapter will focus on cross-gender friendships, i.e., friendships occurring between men and women, the first and larger part will concentrate on the differences there are between the friendship experiences of the two genders. An attempt will be made to account for the variations there are by relating friendship patterns to the broader social contexts in which people's lives are structured. As is now being increasingly recognised, gender is a central feature of social and economic organisation. More than any other characteristic, including class and age, gender defines people's social position and identity, and patterns the opportunities and constraints they face. In quite a real sense, and despite rhetoric to the contrary, males and females continue to occupy separate spheres, to have different demands made of them and consequently to develop different skills and abilities. Thus, the argument of this chapter is not that gender differences in friendship behaviour are innate, but that, in line with the general thrust of the book, the different social positions routinely occupied by the two genders tend to lead to their developing different friendship practices.

There is, of course, a danger here of 'reifying' gender differences by underplaying the other factors which shape people's friendships. As emphasised in Chapter 3, in order to analyse friendship satisfactorily it is necessary to examine the range of social and economic factors that pattern an individual's immediate social environment, rather than focusing solely on any particular one. Like all other aspects of social life, friendship is certainly influenced by gender, but exactly in what way depends on the interaction there is with the other factors that collectively shape the personal space for sociability that people have. This needs to be borne in mind in the discussion that follows.

SOCIALISATION

Numerous studies have shown that the socialisation which boys and girls experience is significantly different. By an early age children know their own gender, recognise its social significance and develop appropriate role models. The roots of this knowledge lie in many spheres, including literary and other media representations and the sorts of games children are encouraged or discouraged from playing. Most significant of all, though, in this process, and mediating these other factors, are the various personal relationships in which the child is involved during the course of his or her development. Through the implicit – and sometimes more overt – control exercised within them, these ties, be they with parents, siblings, relatives, minders, teachers and the rest, inform and continually reinforce the child's notions about gender identity. He or she inculcates the unexceptional and taken-for-granted rules and principles of gendered behaviour precisely because these are largely enacted uncritically in the dealings he or she has with these others.

By the same process, the character of the interactions children have with their friends and peers will reflect (and, of course, augment) their evolving gender performance and identity. Thus, studies in both Britain and America have shown that boys tend to have rather larger friendship networks than girls, but that girls tend to be emotionally closer and more intimate with their smaller number of friends than boys are. They appear willing to reveal more about themselves – their feelings, anxieties and concerns – to their friends than boys are (Maccoby and Jacklin, 1974; Hess, 1979; Dickens and Perlman, 1981). To express this slightly differently, the emphasis in boys' relationships with their peers is generally on shared activities and doing things together. In contrast, with girls the emphasis is more expressive than instrumental, focusing on the relationship itself. For them, communicating and disclosing information about themselves plays a far larger part. As Powers and Bultena (1976) suggest, some of these differences are manifested in the different types of sport that boys and girls are encouraged to play. Boys' sports, like football, cricket or rugby, tend to be team-based and require quite large numbers. The most popular sports for girls, on the other hand, such as swimming, gymnastics and even tennis, are much more individual.

Experiences in childhood, of course, do not necessarily exert an influence over practices in adult life. It is quite possible for new patterns to emerge as people's social circumstances, and the situations to which they are party, alter and change. However, this is less likely to happen if the demands made of them in adulthood are broadly consonant with their experiences during the period of primary socialisation. Significantly, as Hess (1979) amongst others has argued, the patterns of friendship occurring in childhood seem to mesh well with the different roles that the genders typically play in later life. As will be discussed more fully below, males generally lead a more 'public' life than females. Their routine work and leisure activities bring them into contact with a relatively wide range of others and requires them to develop cordial, though not necessarily very close, relationships with them. In contrast, women tend to occupy a more 'private' realm and have less opportunity or reason to develop extensive social networks. However, as part of their familial responsibilities they are expected, as Hess rather aptly puts it, to become 'specialists in human relationships' (1979, p.499) and to devote much of their time and energy to servicing the needs of a relatively small number of others, especially members of their families. To this extent, the gendered patterns of friendship occurring in childhood appear to fit well the demands of later life. Under these circumstances it is not surprising that friendship behaviour continues to be shaped in broadly similar ways throughout adulthood.

FRIENDSHIP INVOLVEMENT

In looking at the impact of gender on adult friendships an obvious question to ask concerns the differentials there are in the numbers of friends men and women have. In point of fact, this is a difficult question to answer with any certainty, for three broad reasons. First, as mentioned above, important though gender is, it is only one of the factors shaping the space people have for friendships, so that it would be surprising if there was any simple relationship between the number of friends a person has and his or her gender. Mediating this relationship are all the other factors, like class, occupation, domestic circumstances and so on, which affect an individual's level of social integration. Secondly, there is really rather little research that examines people's full sociable networks, especially in Britain. The few, mainly American, studies there are tend to be relatively small-scale and to concentrate predominantly on close or best friends. Thirdly, and most importantly, the answers obtained to queries about friendship depend very much on the relationship between the definitions of friendship the respondents (as well as the researchers) draw on in the interviews and the way they routinely organise their sociable relationships.

As discussed more fully in Chapter 2, some people, and in particular those with fewer resources, are more likely to limit their sociability to particular contexts and thereby under-report their sociable ties in responding to questions specifically about 'friendship'.

Given all this, it is not surprising that the conclusions reached in research on the differences in the number of friends the genders have is somewhat contradictory. Some of the American research that focuses explicitly on friendship tends to suggest that there are only minor differences in the number of friends men and women have, but different studies point in different directions. For example, in his well-known survey of individuals aged forty-five or over, Booth (1972) found that there was little difference in the average number of friends claimed by his male and female respondents. Significant differences only emerged when class position was considered, with middle-class males reporting more close friendships than women or working-class males. On the other hand, women tended to spend more time with their friends and to confide in them more (Booth, 1972). Fischer and Oliker's (1983) study of the social networks of a large sample from North California, on the other hand, found that men and women had equivalent network sizes, though there were differences across the life and family course. Married men under thirty-six tended to have more friends than married women in this age category, but at later ages this imbalance was reversed, with women having the fuller friendship network (Fischer and Oliker, 1983). In contrast to both these studies, Lowenthal and her colleagues, in a study based in San Francisco, found that women at each age reported more friends than their male equivalents (Lowenthal *et al.*, 1975.) (See Dickens and Perlman, 1981).

The discrepancies there are in such data may simply reflect the variations that occur in friendship matters. However, one also suspects that, in part, the results obtained are a reflection of the practical difficulties that arise in operationalising the concept 'friend'. Certainly, other forms of evidence suggest that men have more wide-ranging networks of sociability than women. Thus, for example, in Britain community and occupational studies have shown that men have more opportunity in their work and leisure to meet with others and to develop friendships of one form or another, though not all of these ties are recognised as close friendships. In contrast, these same studies suggest that working-class women especially lead much more isolated lives and are far more dependent on kin for sociability. (See Allan, 1979, for a review of this literature.) Even though much of this evidence is now quite old, it does suggest that there are major differences in patterns of sociability. In order to assess these matters more fully, it is worth examining male and female friendship separately.

MALE FRIENDSHIPS

On the whole, men appear to be incorporated more extensively than women into formal and informal relationships. The marked division of labour, both in employment and in domestic responsibilities, plays a major part in this. Clearly, there are significant differences within each grouping, but overall men's work not only routinely involves them in relationships with others, but also, by being quite tightly bounded in time, allows space in their lives for leisure participation. In contrast, largely as a result of their domestic and familial obligations, the structure of most women's lives leaves them with rather less time and opportunity to develop and service informal ties. In particular, there is a structural imbalance within marriage, with wives likely to be socially, as well as economically, dependent on their husbands. Men's domination of employment, as evidenced in the persistent gender inequalities in pay and position, results in wage labour continuing to be seen as their primary, if not sole, responsibility within the domestic economy. Moreover, because they are seen as actually earning the money, irrespective of the work wives do in transforming that wage into living standards and providing personal support services, they tend to be seen as having greater rights over this money. (See Allan, 1985, for a fuller discussion of these issues.) In turn, through having the greater resources and opportunities for leisure, men have been able over time to create a range of formal and informal leisure institutions that facilitate the servicing of informal ties. Although the position may be different in the United States, where middle-class women in particular seem to have generated more leisure associations and clubs catering for their own needs, in Britain women have long been disadvantaged in their access to such leisure provision.

Importantly, while in general men have space within their lives for developing and servicing informal relationships, it does not necessarily follow that they will recognise large numbers of others as friends. Aside from significant variations in other aspects of their lives and, of course, in their personalities and interests, the way in which informal relationships are constructed – the rules of relevance (Paine, 1969) applied to them – may not synchronise particularly well with the different elements the concept of 'friendship' embraces. As discussed in Chapter 2, one important aspect of friendship is the purposefulness of the tie. Friends come together through choice rather than circumstance alone. That is, according to the dominant imagery, the special commitment between friends means that they seek each other out and organise their interaction, rather than just leaving it to apparently chance meetings. Yet, many sociable ties, including many work-based ones, are context-bound and dependent on circumstances. Often, interaction would not occur if both parties did not happen to be involved in some common setting. Sociable ties like these may be quite significant in terms of the individual's sense of social integration and participation without ever being regarded as friendships *per se*.

Although the evidence is by no means conclusive, it can be suggested that the distinct roles that women and men typically perform in society, with the different obligations, opportunities and identities they embody, have an impact on the manner in which friendships and other ties of sociability are constructed. In essence, the argument put forward by a number of writers, including Pleck (1976), Hess (1979) and Bell (1981), is that men's position within the social structure tends in the main to encourage the formation of sociable relationships with others, but, at the same time, to restrict the extent to which the self is revealed within them.

Pleck (1976) expresses this well in drawing on the work of Lewin (1948) and Douvan and Adelson (1966). He suggests that a distinction can be made between *sociability* and *intimacy,* with men's relationships tending to score highly on the former, but relatively low on the latter. Men, in other words, are likely to be involved in a set of relationships whose basis is sociability and enjoyment, often arranged around specific tasks and activities. However, the majority, though not all, of these relationships are likely to be relatively shallow in terms of the degree to which personal worries, anxieties and other matters of consequence to the self are discussed. To this extent, they differ significantly from the 'strong' model of friendship that philosophers abstract, and as importantly also fit somewhat uneasily into the category of 'close friends' so frequently referred to in sociological surveys. In contrast, women's friendships tend to be less extensive and less concerned with sociability as such, but to involve greater self-revelation and empathy, in line with the gender differences in childhood and adolescent friendships noted earlier (Caldwell and Peplau, 1982; Fox, Gibbs and Auerbach, 1985; Rubin, 1986).

While the writers who argue this way are concerned principally with the United States, the image presented seems quite compatible with the portrayal of men's friendship ties found in much British social research. Here, too, there is little evidence in ethnographies or surveys (or, for that matter, in other sources such as fictional or autobiographical accounts), that men's social relationships typically involve very much intimacy or self-disclosure. As Hess (1979) has suggested, such patterns of friendship seem quite highly adapted to the demands that men's roles make of them in industrial societies. Men are supposed to be strong and self-sufficient, able to get along well with a range of others, yet not become dependent on them. At least some of their careers demand mobility, so that the capacity to generate (and, of course, break off) ties with others has some utility. Furthermore, in some respects, there is a tension between cooperation and competition, friendliness and self-interest within the occupational sphere, so that a form of friendship which entails strong elements of non-intimate fellowship appears well-suited.

Perhaps more important than the direct fit between forms of friendship and the needs of a competitive, bureaucratic economy is the articulation of friendship patterns with gender images and identities (Bell, 1981). While stereotypes are easy to ridicule, there is a very definite sense in which men are expected and, indeed, encouraged to display a strength of character which is premised upon a relative absence of sensitivity and the ability to disguise and ignore more tender and compassionate feelings. In other words, while 'harder' emotions like anger and aggression are legitimate, in most contexts the standard construction of male identity serves to limit the extent to which other more caring emotions can be displayed. While some men's perceptions of the damage this restriction on self-expression can have on their psyche have certainly altered in recent years, the dominant paradigm of masculinity continues to disparage any display of what are seen as feminine characteristics or traits.

Thus, notions of male identity can be seen to pattern the friendships men have, but in turn those relationships play their part in sustaining those notions of maleness. Given the dominant images there are of what being masculine entails, it is not surprising that ties of friendship between males are based around sociability rather than intimacy. As Pleck (1976) and Bell (1981) both argue, because of the way masculinity is constructed, there exists a premium against too much self-disclosure in friendships, with the consequence that even apparently close friends do not necessarily confide in each other or discuss personal problems or anxieties. Like the college students studied by Lewis, most men seem to talk 'very little of themselves, their feelings, or their relationships with significant others' (Lewis, 1978, p.116, quoted in Bell, 1981, p.82). Paul Wright (1982) expresses this aptly in suggesting that whereas women's friendships tend to be 'face-to-face' relationships, men's sociable ties are, on the whole, better characterised as 'side by side'. This is likely to be particularly so with less close friends where action rather than intimacy will dominate even more. Here the emphasis on doing things, often in group settings rather than in dyads, especially where the relationships are context-bound rather than more free-floating, helps to structure the setting so that intimate matters are ruled out of court. Furthermore, the bantering, kidding and needling that usually occur on such occasions tend to reinforce this effective moratorium on self-disclosure.

On the whole, then, it could be argued that men are more likely to meet whatever needs they have for intimacy within their families, rather than with their friends and peers. Such a view would be in accord with a great deal of the theorising – both academic and everyday – about the shift in recent generations towards companionate marriage and the privatisation of domestic life. However, as numerous writers have pointed out, it is easy to romanticise the extent to which there has been real change in family organisation. (For a discussion of these issues see Allan, 1985.) Even if men are now better able to express their feelings and emotions within the family context than previously – not least perhaps in their relationships with their young children – the implications of this for gender roles within marriage should not go unheeded. To the extent that men do use their relationships with their wives to express their more personal feelings, anxieties, and worries – and this, of course, is more true of some marriages than others – then, in effect, they are simply endorsing traditional marital roles. In essence, by acting as a principal vessel for emotional expression, these wives are drawing on their expertise in human relations to service their husbands' needs and provide them with support, as writers as different as Parsons (1956), Finch (1983) and Delphy (1984) would recognise.

FEMALE FRIENDSHIPS

Overall, as already mentioned, women's lives are more privatised than men's. Their position within the social structure tends to provide them with less space for leisure and fewer opportunities for social participation. The most obvious factor at work here is the extent to which women's routine obligations for domestic servicing impinge on and constrain other aspects of their lives. On the surface, those most affected here are full-time housewives with responsibility for child care. Aside from being repetitive and monotonous, their work is characterised by the absence of pay and exceptionally long and fragmented hours (Oakley, 1974; Boulton, 1983; Allan, 1985). As a result of the way this work is socially structured, the opportunities and resources women in this situation have for meeting with others, especially outside the child care context, are severely curtailed. Indeed, this tendency has been exacerbated by recent improvements in housing conditions. With fewer people now having to share household amenities or use communally provided facilities, including local shops, there is less scope for meeting casually with others in the neighbourhood. It is consequently not surprising that full-time housewives regularly report having few social contacts and feeling quite isolated and depressed.

Clearly, though, it is not just full-time housewives and mothers whose social lives are affected by domestic responsibilities. As various studies have now demonstrated, the increasing employment of married women, either full-time or part-time, has done little to undermine the conventional division of domestic labour. Whatever their employment status, most wives continue to have by far the major responsibility for housework, meal production and whatever child care tasks need to be done (Hunt, 1980; Pollert, 1981; Gamarnikow *et al.*, 1983; Porter, 1983). They also, of course, bear most of the burden for providing domestic services for elderly parents who can no longer manage adequately for themselves (Finch and Groves, 1980; Nissel and Bonnerjea, 1982). Indeed, despite the significance her earnings now have for the family economy (Coyle, 1984; Pahl, 1984; Yeandle, 1984), in most households the assumption continues to be made that the wife's foremost responsibility is the provision of domestic service. In most cases her employment is fitted in with this, rather than in any way superseding it. In consequence, while employed wives have greater financial independence, many do not have a great deal more time for leisure or for meeting with friends. Indeed, the opposite may be the case, with the 'double burden' of domestic and paid work resulting in their having quite rushed schedules (Sharpe, 1984).

Thus, despite the changes there have been in the social position of women over the last two or three generations, the majority continue to have less space in their lives for leisure and less opportunity for engaging in sociable relationships than most men. Clearly, there are significant differences between different women in these respects. Aside from their diverse domestic responsibilities, the various other factors that shape their immediate social environment, including their financial position, their occupational situation, their level of geographical mobility, their access to transport, and so on, will all play their part in patterning their sociability. The extent to which leisure activities are shared with a husband will also be of consequence, with women in more segregated marriages likely to be amongst the least involved in non-kin sociable networks. Yet, without underplaying the importance of other facets of male dominance, like men's control of many leisure arenas or the risks women face of being attacked if out alone at night, it is the centrality of domestic labour in most women's lives, reinforced by, and in turn reinforcing, the sustained and systematic gender inequalities of the labour market, that is principally responsible for constraining their opportunities for social integration.

Thus, the majority of women are likely to develop fewer informal contacts and relationships than most men. The structural circumstances of their lives are such as to give them less opportunity to become involved in such relationships. This, of course, does not mean that they will necessarily have fewer friends as such, because only a portion of informal contacts are ever transformed into relationships which are recognised as friendships. On the other hand, it would appear from the research literature that some women actually have very few friends and instead build their social lives around ties of kinship. In particular, many community studies of established working-class localities argue that for women with relatively segregated marriages, kin relationships are far more significant in their lives than non-kin ones. This is especially likely to be so if the home is defined as a private space reserved principally for family.

The tendency has been to see these patterns as largely a functional adaptation to the problems of poverty. While this is certainly important, these patterns further demonstrate a degree of male control over female lives. Rather like the 'traditional' male insistence that wives should not be employed, but spend their time at home servicing the needs of husband and family, so, too, the limitation of effective sociable networks to kin relationships is indicative of social arrangements in which women are given rather little personal freedom or space. Even though, at an individual level, these arrangements may be chosen as the preferred way, their social significance is part of the broader canvas of gender inequality, just as the restrictions placed on women's movements and relationships in other cultures are.

Similarly, the conventional images and stereotypes there are of the nature of women's friendships need to be interpreted within the general framework of women's social location. Amongst the most commonly held is the view that women are 'bitchy' about each other, spend their time gossiping and are generally not to be trusted in the way men can be. Furthermore, women's friendships are often portrayed as being rather trivial and of less moment that men's. In general, as Seiden and Bart (1976) point out, popular stereotypes contain some grains of truth, though that truth is usually masked in a fashion that favours the interests of more powerful groupings.

Thus it is with these images of female friendship. At one level much of the content of female friendship – the issues discussed, the topics that unite them – are, from a traditional male perspective, quite trivial. They are about the concerns that dominate many females' lives – domestic and familial matters – just as men's conversation is dominated by their usually equally mundane interests (Bell, 1981). If these topics are seen as trivial it is because men have been successful in defining (and holding) the more socially esteemed and economically rewarded positions and have consistently undervalued the worth of unpaid domestic servicing.

Similarly, the notion that women gossip about one another and cannot be trusted with confidential information can be seen to derive from their primary social role. Their domestic work involves them in the management of personal relationships, both inside the family and outside it. They are thus likely to have privileged access to information that others may wish to be kept private. Yet any discussion or working through of the issues involved with others, however well-meaning or justified, can, without much difficulty, be interpreted as gossiping. Generally, as Seiden and Bart (1976) recognise, this stereotype of female duplicity serves to undermine the value of women as confidantes and, in its small way, bolster dependence on men by highlighting the latter's greater reliability.

At the same time, this also represents one of the more important characteristics of female friendships: the extent to which women are liable to confide in their friends and disclose personal information. As we have seen, men tend to be more sociably integrated than women, but many of their relationships are rather shallow. In contrast, the majority of women may have fewer sociable ties, but, according to a number of writers, more of those they have are likely to be comparatively intimate (Seiden and Bart, 1976; Hess, 1979; Bell, 1981; Johnson and Aries, 1983). The British evidence for such a claim is, admittedly, rather skimpy, and there are certainly likely to be class differentials in notions of privacy and consequently in the boundaries drawn around different relationships governing the information revealed. Nonetheless, the general thrust of the argument seems persuasive (Willmott, 1987).

To begin with, there is not the incompatibility between intimacy and feminine gender identity that there is with masculine identity. On the contrary, qualities such as closeness, empathy and caring are seen as essentially feminine characteristics. Indeed, generally women are thought to possess a greater propensity for handling 'relationship' issues and to be more concerned about them. This is clearly related to the form of work which dominates much of their lives: domestic labour. As well as servicing physical needs, they are also expected to demonstrate 'expressive' qualities and sustain the smooth functioning and harmony of the home. In addition to a capacity to accommodate one's own desires to the needs and demands of others, this requires the development of an expertise in the understanding and handling of personal relationships that is not so obviously evident in men's personae. What is being suggested here, in other words, is that the female's predominant role within the domestic sphere results in her developing social skills which facilitate intimate expression within friendships. Indeed, because of her role as the emotional support of her family, she is more likely than her husband to need to find her own support outside its bounds and discuss personal issues of concern to her with 'outsiders', be they friends or female kin (Lowenthal and Haven, 1968). Furthermore, to the extent that women's friendships are oriented less around specific activities than are men's sociable ties, it is likely that 'talk' and the discussion of matters of personal consequence play a larger part. In Chapter 1 it was argued that friendship is usually seen as rather peripheral to social organisation. It is, as it were, an added extra that makes life more pleasant but is structurally of little consequence. This is particularly true of female friendships. While it is recognised that men's informal contacts may be used to promote their interests – the old boy network and its equivalent at other levels of the status hierarchy – female ties are usually seen as virtually a personal luxury, having no wider social relevance. Thus, as Seiden and Bart (1976) suggest, not only have academic researchers failed to analyse the function of friendship in female life-styles, but, moreover, our everyday understandings trivialise much female sociability and see it as largely superfluous. Such a perception is clearly related to the dominance of women's domestic role. Because this work is privatised and does not, as it is normally organised, encourage cooperative activities, any sociability occurring within it appears to be quite extraneous to its performance and consequently of no real significance. Popular images, however inaccurate they may be, of housewives idly gossiping over the gatepost or spending their time chatting over coffee or tea, reflect the low level of esteem in which these relationships are held. Importantly, it is not just males who trivialise and devalue women's friendships. Many women also appear to underplay the significance of female-female friendships within women's lives (Seiden and Bart, 1976).

Yet there are strong grounds for asserting that non-domestic informal ties of a 'primary' form (Bates and Babchuk, 1961; Lee, 1964) are quite crucial to many women's well-being. Somewhat ironically, a major reason for this is the relative lack of public sociable and leisure outlets catering specifically for women. In the absence of settings in which looser, situationally limited forms of sociable relationships can be developed, more purposeful ties with specific individuals are necessarily more central. However, the social significance of these ties does not lie solely in the realm of sociability and leisure. In line with the arguments of Chapter 4, they are also important because they can act as a flexible resource that enables women to cope better with the demands their domestic role makes of them. Here Eugene Litwak's (1985) recognition that much social organisation is dependent on the ability of informal relationships to 'oil the wheels' of bureaucracies and handle haphazard contingencies as they arise is most pertinent.

As already argued, the articulation of family life with the requirements of the external, non-domestic world is still principally achieved by assigning females – wives and mothers – responsibility for coordination. Their role in the home is not just that of cook, cleaner or child carer, but the fuller, yet more ephemeral, one of domestic servicer. From a societal viewpoint, a major advantage of the role lies in its flexibility to meet the changing physical and emotional needs of other family members and to coordinate these with the varying demands that different organisations and agencies make, haphazardly or otherwise, of the family (Allan, 1985). Yet, as Litwak has long asserted, it is easier to cope with the unexpected contingencies all families at times face if others outside the family can also be called on for help as necessary. Indeed, more generally, it can be argued that women – and not least those who combine domestic responsibilities with paid work – will be better able to handle the range of tasks domestic servicing entails if they can arrange some coordination of effort and exchange of assistance with others.

Of course, to some degree this clashes with the privatised organisation of much domestic servicing. As well as hindering the development of cooperative relationships, there is quite a powerful ideological commitment to many aspects of family business being contained within the family. Yet this, too, indicates the importance of more intimate sociable contacts for women as, in contrast to the situation of most other workers, the absence of a work-based peer group means that such sociable contacts are the main resource available with whom to discuss 'work-related' problems. In other words, it is not just their availability for coping with specific contingencies that makes friendship a significant tie within the structure of many women's lives, but also their availability as a source of support and advice in an otherwise rather isolated role. The possibility of working through different issues with others who share similar values and experiences is especially important, as the demands that domestic servicing makes are not static. In the short term, new contingencies arise that call for new coping strategies, while in the longer run, household organisation has to adapt to the fresh problems generated as its members' needs alter over time.

Plainly, the individuals providing support in these ways need not necessarily be friends. As is evident from numerous community and kinship studies, close female kin – mothers, sisters and daughters –

are also often involved, particularly, though not exclusively, in working-class families. However, such kin may not always be available, whether through demography, geographical mobility or their own commitments. Moreover, many women may regard it as inappropriate to discuss some issues with kin. The kin may, for example, be the source of the problem, or they may be felt to have no experience or understanding of the matter in hand. Or, of course, friends may simply be preferred as confidantes, being chosen because of their compatibility, rather than being ascribed. However, in a sense, the contrast between kin and non-kin is secondary. The crucial issue is that friendship should not be seen as a peripheral relationship within the structure of women's lives. On the contrary, given the routine pattern of family organisation and the dominance of domestic responsibilities within most women's life-styles, informal ties of friendship can be seen to be of major importance. Paradoxical though it may seem, friendships are functional for the successful performance of their role, even though that role of itself provides few opportunities for developing such ties.

CROSS-GENDER FRIENDSHIPS

So far in this chapter the focus has, by implication at least, been on same-gender friendships. In this section the concern will be with friendships between males and females. However, relationships which are predominantly romantic or sexual in orientation will be excluded from the discussion, as the sexual element rather alters the basis of the solidarity involved. Similarly, notwithstanding the claim some make that their spouses are their best friends, marital ties will also be excluded, as they, too, clearly involve a different level of commitment than friendship as normally understood.

Even by the general standards of friendship research, the literature on cross-gender friendships is extremely sparse. While this reflects the relative infrequency of dyadic cross-gender friendships, it is rather surprising that friendships between couples have not received more attention, given the ideological emphasis placed on companionship within marriage and the place of couple relationships within social life. Much of the material that is available is now quite dated. However, it is evident that a good proportion of some couples' closer friendships are couple-oriented. There is, of course, much variation in the extent to which this is so. Many studies have shown it is likely to be least true of working-class sociability and most true of middle-class forms. The issue raised in Chapter 2 about the extent to which the home is used to socialise with non-kin is likely to be relevant here, though overall the most crucial influence is likely to be the nature of the marital bond itself. Where, in Bott's (1971) terms, a couple have a predominantly joint marital role, their friendships are likely to reflect this and to some degree be shared. More segregated marital roles are likely to lead to fewer shared friendships, even where they are associated with more dense networks.

This, of course, raises the issue of what exactly a couple friendship implies. The normal criterion is that the two couples socialise with each other as couples, rather than predominantly as individuals. Yet this does not necessarily mean that the friendship ties between the four of them are equivalent or equally strong. In some instances this may be so, but culturally the expectation appears to be that the closest relationships will be between the two males and the two females rather than cutting across gender boundaries. In the absence of studies examining such friendships in detail, the evidence is anything but systematic. Nonetheless, it would seem that same-gender ties within couple relationships are in practice emphasised more than the cross-gender ones, though this may not always be recognised (Babchuk, 1965). So, for example, it is far more common for the two females or the two males within such couple friendships to meet without their partners or go out somewhere together than it is for the cross-gender pairs from the two couples to socialise independently. Similarly, where separate conversations develop, it is more likely to involve same-gender pairings than the male and female from the different couples. To this extent, many couple relationships may, in fact, have more in common with same-gender friendships than they do with cross-gender ones, though this argument is hard to sustain in the absence of reliable empirical material. Hence, in what follows, the focus will be more on individual cross-gender friendships than on couple-based ones.

While cross-gender friendships are comparatively rare, as with other forms of friendship, the extent to which they occur is, in part, a consequence of the opportunities open to individuals to meet with people of the other gender within a context which facilitates the development of these relationships (Booth and Hess, 1974). In other words, as before, one issue that matters here is the nature of the individual's immediate social environment and the space this provides for instigating and servicing cross-gender relationships of a non-sexual character. There will, of course, be a good deal of variation in this. To begin with, the individual's structural location will play some part. Thus, for example, because of their different leisure patterns, the young and single may have easier contact with potential friends of the opposite gender than, say, the majority of married people with domestic and child care responsibilities. In addition, more contingent factors are likely to affect the opportunities an individual has to develop cross-gender sociable ties. For example, some occupations and work settings – those in which gender does not figure large in the division of responsibility and labour – will do more than others to encourage cross-gender friendships. Similarly, as suggested above, the organisation of some marriages will foster such ties more than others.

Yet, while structural and situational factors will affect the opportunities individuals have for generating and sustaining cross-gender friendships, their importance is more than matched by the normative constraints which discourage the formation of friendships across gender lines. As discussed at the beginning of this chapter, gender is arguably the most pervasive feature of social organisation. From an early age people learn to attribute gender and relate to males and females in discrete ways. Further, as Bell (1981) argues, the tendency for men and women to characterise and respond to each other in terms of sexual attractiveness, whether or not this is consciously recognised, means that elements of sexuality often impinge on cross-gender sociability from the outset.

To put this another way round, while we are extensively socialised into appropriate ways of behaving in same-gender friendships, we are, if anything, socialised away from cross-gender friendships. There are relatively few cultural representations or guidelines about how to organise them in an asexual or non-romantic fashion. Instead, the dominant models for sociable interaction between the genders are based upon a more or less overt sexuality. As a consequence, when people of the opposite gender enter into a sociable relationship in their own right, it is frequently taken to involve some level of sexual interest, rather than being straight-forward friendship (Adams, 1985).

Because of the intrusion of aspects of sexuality, then, cross-gender friendships tend to be rather different from same-gender ones. To begin with, the pattern of interaction between such friends may have sexual undercurrents, with cross-gender friendships often incorporating at least tacit recognition of a sexual dimension and an affirmation of sexual identity (Rubin, 1985). For instance, even in couple relationships, flirting and sexual innuendo commonly serve this purpose, though they are often expressed in a consciously joking form so as to render them innocent (Bell, 1981). Furthermore, there is the potential within cross-gender friendships for a more active sexual relationship to develop. Where this does occur the basis of the solidarity of the friendship is altered and usually it is difficult to revert to the previous state once the sexual relationship ends.

Perhaps most importantly, cross-gender friendships differ from same-gender ones in the extent to which others attempt to influence and control them. Conventionally, friendship is supposed to be a personally free relationship, so that choice of friends and what is done with them is, within broad legal and moral limits, a matter for the individuals involved to determine. In reality, of course, all friendships are social as well as personal constructions, patterned to some degree by convention as well as the demands of others. This, however, is especially true of cross-gender friendships, where the possibility of sexual involvement often leads to more intrusive social pressure and informal control being exercised. Whether expressed as jealousy, gossip or disapproval, the reaction of others – real or conjectured – is likely to have a greater influence on cross-gender friendships than on same-gender ones. Indeed, the infrequency of such ties and the relative absence of accepted conventions on which to base them is itself an effective form of discouragement.

However, as Bell (1976) argues, there are some situations in which cross-gender friendships are more likely to develop. In these situations the potential sexuality of the relationship is rendered 'safe' by the way it is structured. An example already mentioned is the involvement of people in couple relationships where the presence of partners sustains a largely asexual definition of the ties. A second example is the friendships between colleagues which are framed by the work context. A third is friendships in which there is a large age difference, like the ones that Adam's (1985) elderly female respondents reported having with younger men who helped them out in one way or another. At issue here is the way that the contexts in which these relationships are constructed tend to counter any sexual implication and establish their status as legitimate friend-ships. Of course, some of these friendships do lead to sexual liaisons, but the point is that asexual cross-gender friendships can develop when circumstances are structured so as to minimise the relevance and impact of the sexual dimension.

In summary, the argument of this section has been that for both structural and normative reasons, cross-gender frienships of an asexual form are relatively rare. Throughout much social life the divisions between the genders are such as to limit the opportunities there are for forming these friendships. It is far more common to associate sociably with people of the same gender. In addition, the issue of sexuality systematically intrudes into cross-gender friendships, not just at a personal level but also because socially there is little institutional or informal support given to these ties. A question that obviously arises is whether this will alter very much over the next generation or two. Adams (1985), in her discussion of the absence of such ties amongst her elderly population, suggests that cross-gender friendships are more likely to emerge among younger cohorts as a consequence of their different experiences. To the extent that gender segregation has become less pronounced in a range of social institutions, so that the genders have more opportunity to meet sociably and have fewer controls exercised over their contacts, this seems possible.

On the other hand, it is clear that gender remains a principal basis of social organisation and continues to affect sociability quite markedly. Friendship patterns continue to be largely gender-specific amongst all age groups, with relatively few cross-gender friendships reported. Where they do arise, they tend to be seen by those involved, as well as by others, as rather different from the same-gender friendships they sustain. Most important, there is little evidence that cross-gender friendships, especially outside a couple context, are becoming that much more socially legitimated. They are certainly not taken for granted in the way same-gender ties are, nor have they been routinely incorporated into leisure and other sociable organisation. Clearly, there are likely to be occupational and class differences in this, with some professional workers, for example, more likely to develop cross-gender friendships as a consequence of their work situations. Overall though, despite the changes there have undoubtedly been, it seems unlikely that there will be radical shifts in the gendered pattern of friendship. Same-gender friendships will continue to dominate until gender itself becomes an insignificant dimension of social experience.

6

FRIENDSHIP IN OLD AGE

From a sociological perspective the most interesting research on friendship over the last ten years has been concerned with friendship amongst elderly people. More consistently than in any other field of friendship research, the focus has been on the way in which the individual's circumstances pattern his or her friendship involvement and on the social and personal significance of friendship in that person's life. However the bulk of this research is American, with British research on elderly people being far less concerned with the part played by informal relationships in elderly people's well-being. As Dorothy Jerrome (1981), the major exception to this generalisation, notes, British studies have developed little since the now classic work of Peter Townsend and his colleagues in the 1950s and early 1960s. In consequence, this chapter will draw quite heavily on American research. In so doing it is not being assumed that British experience will mirror American patterns in any simple fashion. Rather, the strength of the American work to be discussed in this chapter is that it recognises that friendship is a social, rather than simply a personal, relationship and consequently poses the sorts of question about informal ties that were developed in previous chapters.

The traditional image of elderly people is of a dependent group whose horizons become narrowed as the opportunities they have for social and economic involvement gradually diminish. In Rosow's somewhat exaggerated terms, elderly people's lives become 'socially unstructured, essentially vague, devoid of socially defined objectives . . . In so far as *social* personality consists of the complex of one's roles, the loss and ambiguity of role expectations seriously undermine their very social identity' (1967, p.254, quoted in Jerrome, 1981, p.176). Whether such disengagement is seen as primarily consequent upon organisational practice, as with retirement, or infirmity or illness, or even personal disposition, matters little. The result is that elderly people are assumed to lack the degree of social integration normal for most other adults. Within this context, friendship may become particularly significant. Without other more formal means of social participation, elderly people become increasingly reliant upon informal contacts with friends and kin for reinforcing their social identity and giving shape to their self-image. However, precisely because their institutional involvement is reduced, the opportunities they have for generating and servicing friendships are themselves limited. Moreover, their network of friends is likely to be decreasing as their friends become infirm or, indeed, die.

Such a portrayal of the elderly population is misleading, to say the least. To begin with, they are not the homogeneous group this imagery implies. While the social and physical conditions of ageing foster some similarity, the divisions there are amongst elderly people are certainly of greater importance. Age itself is a major basis of division, as increased life expectancy this century has resulted in the category 'elderly' covering a very wide age span. The life style of a healthy sixty-five-year-old is likely to have as much, if not more, in common with someone of forty-five than someone of eighty-five, never mind one hundred and five. But, even if the elderly population is divided into different age cohorts, the differences and divisions between their experiences, past and present, remain. Aside from the pervasive influence of gender, their different material resources – in particular, their occupational and state pension rights and their housing circumstances – are bound to influence the pattern of their activities. So, too, while linked with economic position, the relative health or infirmity of elderly people creates divisions between them that are not just a correlative of chronological age. In a nutshell, while each cohort has the past in common, the legacy of that past on current circumstances and the consequent relationship between age and social activities show far greater variety than our popular stereotypes allow. With friendship, as with other matters, it is inappropriate to construct theories about ageing's effects that fail to recognise the non-uniformity of the process.

Because the social situation of elderly people is variable, so, too, are the opportunities they have to develop and sustain different friendships. In line with what was said in Chapter 3, the constraints that ageing imposes on friendship patterns are not determined by age *per se*, but differ from individual to individual, depending on their immediate social environment and the constellation of their circumstances. There will certainly be factors, like class, gender and indeed age, which structure these patterns, but they do not do so in the distinctly mechanical fashion assumed in much survey research into the elderly population's friendships. Obviously, there will be some elderly people whose personal situation is such that servicing friendships is extremely difficult (Wenger, 1984). Those individuals who are housebound are particularly likely to find that with time their circle of friends and acquaintances diminishes, though, for some, telephoning or letter writing can provide a means of maintaining contact. Others may find their friendships eroded by the demands that caring for an incapacitated spouse or parent makes of them. (The effect of such caring on friendship patterns will be discussed more fully in the next chapter.)

For the majority of elderly people, however, opportunities for socialising with others and maintaining friendships are built into their routines. Some avenues, such as employment, may be closed off by age, but others continue to provide a mechanism for servicing sociable relationships. Leisure associations of one form or another are likely to be particularly important, and they, of course, do not discriminate rigidly by age. Many elderly people may now have more time to participate in different leisure pursuits – or 'social worlds' in Unruh's (1983) terms – than at other stages in their life when work or family responsibilities dominated their activities. Although there appear to be no specific studies of this, it could be that the 'young old' play an important part in the running of the range of voluntary and leisure associations found in every locality, as was the case in a number of the neighbourhood care schemes Philip Abrams studied (Bulmer, 1986). Of course, the extent to which leisure organisations are significant in the lives of elderly people is likely to bear some relationship to the levels of their participation in earlier stages of their lives. Certainly, some elderly people will be less able or willing than others to join leisure associations, of whatever form. Nonetheless, meeting people through taking up new activities and pastimes represents for many an important means of developing and servicing sociable contacts (Unruh, 1983).

This is a matter discussed fully by Jerrome (1981) in her analysis of the importance of friendship in the lives of sixty-six older, mainly 'unattached' women. Amongst other issues, she considers the different strategies these women use to maintain and develop their friendship circles. Joining clubs, societies and associations of one sort or another was one of the main strategies used, with nearly all the women in the study belonging to at least one voluntary association. Membership of these clubs and societies did not necessarily generate close friendships of an intimate form – a source of disappointment to some – but they did provide a forum for meeting other people and socialising on a more casual level. Such friendships are likely to dissipate if, for whatever reason, interaction in the club context ceases, but this does not mean that these relationships are of limited social significance. The boundaries around them may be defined rather narrowly, but they still serve the function of integrating the individual into a wider social milieu. Interestingly, the form of club that appears to be least successful in this respect is that created with the specific aim of generating friendships. As Hart (1976) also found in her study of the separated and divorced, clubs which make the function of friendship formation explicit serve to highlight the apparent social inadequacy of those who need to depend on them. By not having some other rationale, be it card-playing, charitable work, religious commitment or whatever, friendship clubs make the development of sociable relationships appear forced and, to this extent, 'unnatural'.

Of course, clubs and other voluntary associations are not the only mechanism available for sustaining friendship networks. While work-based relationships are likely to be affected by retirement, an individual's other friendship and sociable contacts are not necessarily going to alter radically when he or she reaches sixty-five or any other age. Unless there is geographical mobility at this time, most will continue. One strategy that many of Jerrome's respondents used for extending their friendship circles was to build on existing relationships and develop them into closer friendships than they have previously been. In the main, this either involved reactivating relationships that had for whatever reason become attenuated over time, or else cultivating what had previously been just acquaintances into more fully fledged friendships. Thus, Jerrome reports that new friendships were formed in her sample with ex-colleagues, previous neighbours and even the parents of children's friends. Essentially, the personal space that these women had for friendship in old age facilitated and encouraged the transformation of these relationships into friendships at this time in a fashion that circumstances or predisposition had not previously allowed.

The importance of Jerrome's work is that it emphasises both the significance of friendship ties in old age and the extent to which people can accrue as well as lose friendships at this phase in their lives. This latter point is developed further by Rebecca Adams (1987) in an important paper on network change which accords well with the framework discussed in Chapter 3. Like Jerrome, Adams studied the friendship patterns of older 'unattached' women, living, in her case, in a middle-class suburb of Chicago. Half the women in her sample lived in age-segregated housing complexes and half elsewhere in the community (Adams, 1986). Her main study was undertaken in 1981, but in 1984 she reinterviewed forty-two of her original sample of seventy. Even within these three years, she discovered that there had been significant change in the composition of the friendships of her sample, changes which, as Adams argues, were probably continuations of processes begun earlier. On average they nominated more friends in 1984 than in 1981, more of these friends lived nearby, and their friendship networks were denser. On the other hand, they apparently saw less of these friends and felt emotionally more distant from them.

While these findings are interesting in that they run counter to the dominant image of friendship change in old age, presenting the data in this aggregated form is also a little misleading, as it hides important variations within the sample, variations which are consequent on the past and present life styles of the respondents. Adams divides her sample into three status groups which she terms: 'members of high society'; 'pillars of the community'; and 'marginal women' (1987, p.224). 'Members of high society' tended to have higher incomes than the others, to look younger than their age and wear higher quality clothing, to belong to literary and other culturally oriented societies and to come from smaller families. Between the two studies the friendship networks of women in this category had contracted, but the friendships they had were emotionally stronger. What, in other words, had happened was a 'culling' of their more casual friendships. As Adams notes, this culling process can best be understood in terms of the context of these women's lives. Many had maintained casual friendships through their own or their husbands' professional and business pursuits. There was a sense of constraint about these more casual friendships; to an extent, they were necessary for other purposes and not freely chosen. Now that they had retired or, being widowed, no longer had to concern themselves with their husbands' priorities, these women felt free to concentrate on more meaningful friendships. Thus, their sociable circles had decreased, but had done so in a way that, from their viewpoint, represented something of a qualitative 'improvement'.

In contrast, the friendship networks of the 'pillars of the community' group had tended to expand through involving proportionately more non-local friendships. These women tended to have lived longer in the area, to have worked locally if they had been employed and to belong to local clubs and churches. Generally, they had been quite tied to the locality through their children or husbands, or through their own employment. During the three years between the interviews, these women seemed to have replaced some of their local contacts with friendships with people from outside the neighbourhood. Being more free of obligation than before, they were able to expand their friendship horizons and cultivate new relationships or ones that had previously been somewhat dormant.

The final group of women Adams identifies, the 'marginal women', tended to be less securely middle-class than the other two groups. They had lower incomes, made more use of social services and belonged to fewer organisations. They had also moved more frequently than most of the other women in the sample and lived in the area for a shorter time. Overall, their friendship circles had expanded over the three years, principally through the addition of a number of more casual local friends. In middle age these women had not had the resources to develop very extensive networks of friends. While in retirement they still did not belong to that many clubs, they did participate in the various recreation centres for elderly people that existed in the locality. This had enabled them to get to know a relatively wide range of others, albeit within bounded contexts, and thus expand their sociable networks (Adams, 1987).

Both Jerrome's and Adams's samples consisted principally of middle-class single, divorced or widowed females with a relatively wide age spread. As such, it would clearly be inappropriate to assume the patterns they uncovered were in any sense representative of the elderly population more generally. The friendships of elderly people with other social and economic characteristics are likely to be quite different. Indeed, in a sense, this is the main point to be drawn from these analyses. What they demonstrate very clearly is that friendships are not just passively dissipated in old age, as many models of the ageing process imply, just as they are not in other life phases, but altered and changed in accordance with the overall social positions of those concerned. Other things being equal, especially health, elderly people are involved in an active reconstruction of their friendship networks in ways shaped by the freedoms and constraints of their current situation, i.e. in the language of Chapter 3, their 'immediate social environment' or 'personal space'.

The link between friendship patterns and an individual's immediate social environment is brought out particularly clearly in Adams's study. Even though this covers only a very short time span – three years – she is nonetheless able to illustrate the sort of incipient change that friendship networks undergo as people's social position alters, and relate these quite directly to the shifts in role, opportunity and obligation that the individual is experiencing or has experienced. Adams suggests that the changes occurring in her respondents' friendship networks can be seen as something of a 'reversal' of the patterns dominant during their middle years. While this may be true with respect to many of the women in her sample, reversal of previous patterns is not an inevitable outcome of old age, any more than it is at other times when one's social position alters. The process is more one whereby the patterns of friendship established at different times are linked to the overall constellation of commitments and opportunities affecting the individual. Thus, had Adams or Jerrome studied some other group, the details of how their networks were changing and of the strategies the individuals used with respect to friendship ties would be different. They would, nonetheless, be shaped by those individuals' immediate social environments, just as the friendship changes within Adams's three status groups were predicated by their current circumstances and their past experiences. The absence of any need to socialise with their own or their husbands' colleagues or other business contacts, the ready availability of social clubs, the reduction of local commitments, or whatever, led to the development of new friendship patterns at this time in their lives, in much the same way as the absence of these conditions helped shape their previous friendship strategies and outcomes.

To underline an earlier point, what is made particularly evident in these studies is the inadequacy of relying on simple 'macro' level variables for understanding friendship patterns. Attempts to analyse friendship in terms of age, say, or class, or gender, or marital status or whatever, are too gross to be very useful. It is the interplay of the range of factors which structures and constrains the options and choices open to an individual that needs considering if the ways in which friendship and other sociable relations are organised are to be understood.

THE SIGNIFICANCE OF FRIENDSHIP FOR ELDERLY PEOPLE

As already noted, there is wide agreement in the research literature that friends are an important resource for the elderly population because of the relative demise of more structured roles in their lives. Not only do friends offer a means of social integration, but they are also able to provide each other with practical and emotional support of different forms, depending on their particular needs and circumstances. Moreover, friends help one another to come to terms with old age and provide a continuing validation of self, at a time when other indicators of individual worth are less prominent. Furthermore, as Hess (1972) has argued, friends play a major role in the socialisation of elderly people by helping each other find appropriate ways of adapting to the personal, physical and social changes that occur in this life phase.

While the significance of friendship in the lives of elderly people is evident, it is equally clear that the extent to which a person's friends are able to perform these various functions depends on the nature of the relationships that are maintained. Some friendship networks will be more extensive than others; some will be more localised; some will contain a high proportion of quite long-lasting friendships; in others, relatively shallow ties will dominate; and so on. This has led to attempts by a number of writers to specify the variations there are in friendship patterns and to link these to other facets of elderly people's lives. For example, on the basis of interviews with a small, heterogeneous sample of elderly people, Sarah Matthews (1983) distinguishes between two different conceptions of friendship. In the first, the emphasis is on the particular individual who is the friend; in the second, the focus is more on the relationship as such. As she recognises, the distinction here is largely between those closer friendships which cannot be easily replaced, and those less intimate ones which, being defined as more dependent on circumstances, can more readily be replaced by a substitute. In a later publication, Matthews (1986) concentrates less on the character of particular friendships and more on the overall strategies individuals adopt in shaping their friendship networks. Here she identifies three different friendship styles: the independents, who claimed few friends as such; the discerning, who recognised a small number of very close friends; and the acquisitive, who had a broader conception of friendship and felt committed, for the present at least, to a larger circle of acquaintances. In a somewhat similar fashion, Adams (1986), in the study cited earlier, distinguishes between a primary orientation to friendship and a secondary orientation. As with Matthews's 'discerning' style, a primary orientation is one in which friendship is taken to be a rather exclusive, intimate relationship that develops with only a few others. A secondary orientation, on the other hand, is a much more catholic, inclusive one, in which virtually everyone with whom one socialises is regarded as a friend.

As well as representing different approaches to sociability, the broad distinctions being made here reflect the different boundaries that are drawn around the concept of 'friend'. That is, some people require more of a relationship for it to qualify as a friendship (at least in an interview setting), than others. It is important to recognise that having a secondary orientation to friendship does not mean that no qualitative distinctions are made between one's various friends. In Matthews's terms, the majority of the acquisitive group have some friendships that are closer and more intimate than the rest – equivalent to the friendships recognised by the 'discerning' – but do not exclude as friends people who do not meet these exacting criteria. Although there are many layers to the bald contrast between close and less close friends, even in this crude form the distinction is a useful one for examining the significance of friendship in the lives of elderly people and the part it plays in their well-being.

Clearly, no necessary correlation exists between the frequency of face-to-face interaction and the closeness of a friendship tie. As discussed in Chapter 2, friendships of different sorts are developed throughout one's life. However, the majority of these friendships do not survive any major changes that occur in either side's circumstances, such as geographical mobility or changed domestic status. Instead, most of the previous sociable ties become inactive, with new relationships being developed to take their place in the friendship circles of those involved. Other things being equal, the only friendships that are likely to continue despite changed circumstances are those which are defined as particularly close. Thus, as a result of routine patterns of mobility over the life course, it is highly likely that many elderly people will not live particularly near to their closest friends and so not see them very frequently. Conversely, while some may have close friends in the immediate vicinity, in many cases those with whom they spend most time may not be the ones to whom they feel closest.

Yet, while an elderly person's most intimate friendships may not be particularly active in this sense, they can still fulfil important functions for the individual precisely because they have been long-lasting. Indeed, the fact that they have survived, where other relationships have not, is itself an indication for those involved of their special strength and quality. The majority are well aware that the solidarity and commitment inherent in these friendships cannot easily be developed in new relationships. They have stood the test of time and now have built into them a form of personal history inevitably missing from new friendships. Old friends knew you as you were. With them the ups and downs of the past can be recalled and lived over again. As Jerrome (1981) argues, there is a sense in which such old friends are thought to know you as you really are, not just as someone who is now growing old, but as someone who has lived a life and experienced all that this involves. In such ways, friends known over the years can help provide meaning and continuity in old age by validating each other's experience and signifying their individuality.

While close friendships which have survived over the years do provide a sense of identity in these ways, in situations where the friends are separated geographically there are clearly limitations on the overall role they can play in each other's lives. They cannot share in many more mundane activities in the way that more local friends can, activities which may be particularly important for the social integration of elderly people and, in turn, for their psychological well-being. While the idea of 'psychological well-being' contains many dimensions, there is broad agreement in the research literature that those elderly people who are relatively well integrated into the wider society are likely to have a higher morale, a better self-image and be more content with their adjustment to ageing (Pihlblad and Adams, 1972; Wood and Robertson, 1978; Adams, 1986).

Obviously, friendships and other informal ties can play a significant part in such integration, not least by providing routine involvement on an everyday basis. In this respect, the existence of a small number of emotionally close friendships may be less significant than involvement with a wider circle of less intimate ties, especially if the close friends happen not to live locally. What appears to matter is not so much having one or two friends with whom one's innermost thoughts can be readily shared, but rather being involved in different social activities that provide opportunities to socialise with others on a more or less regular basis and develop a range of less intimate friendships. Thus, in Adams's (1986) research, those respondents who adopted a secondary orientation to friendship – i.e., who applied wider, less exclusive criteria – were more likely than those with a primary orientation – whose definition of friendship was much narrower – to have a positive sense of well-being. As Adams (1986) points out, having a secondary orientation to friendship does not imply the absence of any emotionally close ties, but simply that other forms of friendship are also recognised and encouraged. In practice, close friends may play a part in helping each other become more socially integrated by, say, introducing one another to a wider circle of friends or accompanying each other to provide support in new ventures. Overall, however, it appears not to be the strength of particular ties that matter here so much as the presence of a wider circle of contacts who serve to provide a fuller sense of participation and belonging. Of course, it must always be remembered that, irrespective of their orientation to friendship, not all elderly people will have the same possibilities of developing a wide circle of friendships and becoming socially integrated in this way. Some, through infirmity, domestic obligation or other constraint, will not be in a position to service a wide range of friendships, nor to lead lives which involve them very fully in the wider society.

FRIENDS AND KIN

Friendships are not the only ties that help to integrate the individual into the social world. For the majority, kinship also plays a role in this. As different studies have shown, in the main it is primary kin – children and siblings – who are most significant in the lives of elderly people, though for some of the childless, a particular nephew or niece may be especially important. Interestingly, though, given some of the assumptions that are sometimes made, there is relatively little evidence that kin and friends can really substitute for one another. Indeed, a good deal of American research argues that overall the two sets of relationships play different functions in the lives of the elderly population. While it is possible that the situation in Britain is somewhat different, and that class-based variations in these patterns are more important than the American literature allows, the basic arguments are persuasive enough to consider more fully.

In general, the relationship between parents and their adult children can be characterised as one of positive concern (Adams 1967). Each side feels a commitment to the other and a moral obligation to provide one another with support when needed. The nature of this support, and its direction, will vary over the life course, depending on the specific circumstances of those involved. When old age generates personal and social dependence, it is routinely children, and in particular a specific daughter or daughter-in-law, who provides care and support (Finch and Groves, 1980; 1983; Equal Opportunities Commission, 1982; Nissel and Bonnerjea, 1982). However, at any time the great majority of elderly people are not in need of this form of support. Rather, their relationship with their children is more likely to be largely social in character, involving fairly regular contacts and visits, knowledge of each other's welfare and, where feasible and appropriate, minor assistance in each other's projects. The relationships, in other words, are premised on a long-standing commitment which is rarely broken. Yet it is important to note that the basis of the relationship is not of itself sociability and enjoyment, notwithstanding the class and gender differences emphasised in traditional kinship studies. Certainly, at times parents and their adult children will engage in sociable activities together, but, unlike the situation in friendships, this is not the underlying rationale for the relationship (Allan, 1979; 1985).

So, while descendent kin, and especially daughters, tend to play a far more significant role than friends in care provision as elderly people become increasingly dependent, in contrast they appear to be less successful as a means of integrating older individuals into the wider society. Thus studies by, for example, Wood and Robertson (1978), Chappell (1983) and G. Lee (1985) suggest that there is little or no correlation between children's visits and the morale of elderly people, but a more direct tie between their morale and interaction with friends. In part, this is a consequence of friendship being defined as a more voluntary, less obligatory relationship than parent-adult child ones. In whatever form it takes, friendship involves people who have chosen to spend time together, evidently on the basis of their liking for and their appreciation of one another's personality and character. While, like close kinship, friendship entails an element of positive concern, it does not involve the same elements of responsibility or duty. As Adams (1967) suggests, the basis lies more in a consensus of values than in moral obligation and debt.

As a consequence, the social and personal significance of interaction with children and friends is quite different. In a sense, having friends and other sociable contacts to interact with signifies social competence, the value of the individual as a person and, for elderly people especially, a continuing independence. In contrast, without other sources of social involvement, interaction with adult children may symbolise what is usually an unwelcome dependence and a lack of wider social valuation. Given the obligatory undercurrents of the relationship, the reversal of its previous exchange basis and its evident imbalance as parents become more dependent, it is not surprising that involvement with adult children appears to have less impact on elderly people's morale and sense of social worth than ties of friendship.

A further reason why friends may be more effective for the morale of elderly people than interaction with adult children is developed by Blau (1973). She suggests that, aside from the obligatory nature of kinship ties, the generational differences in experience and assumed understanding are important. In a sense she is arguing that, apart from kinship itself, there is little to bring the generations together. Friends of a similar age do have a common reference to the present in the past which is likely to generate a common way of interpreting and making sense of the events of the day that concern them. Equally, of course, such friends are likely to share similar interests and occupy similar structural positions, thereby giving them more in common with one another than they have with people of a different generation (Wood and Robertson, 1978).

While these sorts of generational difference appear to be present at all life stages, for elderly people the role of similarly aged friends in cementing a world view and supporting meaning structures may be particularly important, both because of the relative absence of formal role positions to give a sense of direction to their lives and because of the knowledge that time is running out. Under these circumstances the past provides a major point of reference, especially if current social activities become limited. In consequence, being able to reflect on the good and bad times of the past – as well as to discuss current concerns – with age peers is likely to be more important for morale than talking it over with people whose time perspective is very different. As Chappell (1983) argues, siblings may also become significant in old age for similar reasons. They, too, share a time perspective and, of course, a common background. Jerrome's (1981) work is again of interest here because many of those in her sample who were close to their siblings had become so only comparatively recently. In old age they came to have a utility and significance previously less marked.

WIDOWHOOD

A strong case can thus be made for the salience of friendship in old age. Even more so, it can be argued that friends have a major role to play in helping people come to terms with the many emotional and practical problems of widowhood. Clearly, many of the issues already discussed in this chapter are pertinent to the situation in which widows find themselves – indeed a number of the more interesting studies reviewed included widows among their sample. Nonetheless, the role that friends are able to play in helping individuals cope with and adjust to the loss of a spouse, and conversely the impact this loss has on friendship patterns, is worth discussing separately here. To some extent, the issues raised in this section could have been incorporated into Chapter 7, which is explicitly concerned with the consequences for friendship of social change. The discussion is included here as it bears so much on old age, though some of the points to be made will be raised again in the next chapter.

As with old age generally, the popular view is that widowhood tends to limit people's involvement with their friends. Some research lends support to this view, though most emphasises the need to consider other factors apart from widowhood alone. Certainly, the processes involved seem to be more subtle than the basic 'loss of friendship' idea implies. In general there is agreement that widowhood leads to changes in the personnel of friendships, but this does not necessarily entail a reduction in the overall level of contact an individual has with his or, more usually, her friends. What matters, as Zena Blau's (1961) influential analysis first illustrated, is the situation of the widow relative to those by whom she is surrounded. Because of the tendency for structural balance within friendship, in the course of time widows are likely to become less involved with their existing still-married friends and find their friendship circles biased more towards other widows. Consequently, Blau argues, thosed who are widowed early are likely to find themselves relatively isolated because most of their peers are still married. In contrast, those who are widowed nearer the 'average' age of widowhood are less likely to have difficulty generating friendships, as there is a larger pool of other widows available. Indeed, as Blau points out, for the same reasons of structural balance, the still-married are likely to be more isolated in later old age than the widowed, as there will now be fewer other still-married couples surviving. In a broadly similar vein, it can be argued that not only does the age at widowhood matter here, but the 'population density' of widows in the area in which an individual lives is also of consequence. As Petrowsky's (1976) research suggests, where there is a high number of other widows in an area, then generating friendships is going to be easier than where there are few, even if widowhood is experienced relatively early in life. The processes by which 'uncoupled' friendships emerge in widowhood are worth discussing a little more fully. Clearly there is unlikely to be a 'clean break' with still-married friends. Indeed in Lopata's studies, many widows continued to nominate couple friends, while nonetheless recognising that the relationships had altered and that interaction was less frequent (Lopata, 1979). Sometimes contact is lost through geographical mobility, particularly if the widow moves to be nearer to a child. In other cases previous friendships may cease because the primary tie was with the late spouse, rather than the surviving widow. More often, though, the decline of the friendship results from the difficulties both sides experience in carrying on as before under changed circumstances. Maintaining the balance of exchange, and reciprocating equally when the units within the tie are different, presents minor problems and tensions, for which solutions are not readily found. Whether it is a matter of no longer having a common set of everyday experiences, of feeling uncomfortable in some 'couple dominated' social settings, of having difficulty in sustaining the cross-gender tie, of not being sure of the 'rules' that govern reciprocity of exchange, or whatever, the consequence is that these relationships become that much less comfortable and easy than they were previously.

Their problematic tenor was well expressed by one of Matthews's respondents:

'And couples tend to stay with couples. And visit in the home of couples, of course. And I invite them, but it isn't like it used to be when we were a couple. It's a very different life . . . I have friends who swim, but they still have their husbands. Now you see, I don't like to join husband-wife groups. If there were single women going and they said, 'Come on, let's swim,' that would be a different thing. But to me, to make it a point to be over there when they go there, I wouldn't do that. I just wouldn't do it. That's all. I don't know, as a widow you walk a much more careful line in how you do things than when you were married. Life is much prettier and easier when you're a married couple. The places you go, the way you do things, the kind of invitations you give and accept.' (Matthews, 1986, p.118)

Important in this account is the idea that it is not just married friends who reject the widows, but that a subtle, two-way process is at work. Whatever the feelings and intentions of the friend couple, the widow herself evidently feels ill at ease within these relationships and unsure of how to handle them. As a consequence, while still visiting them, she is gradually distancing herself from these friendships and apparently looking for new ties with single people to take their place. Of course, the extent to which this happens, and its speed, will vary. Some people can cope with the strains generated better than others. In some cases too, the friendships may be gradually transformed into a more manageable single gender one (Lopata, 1979). But in many cases the tensions of sustaining asymmetrical relationships are such as to make it easier to allow them to wither.

As with other aspects of ageing, there has until recently been a tendency in much of the literature on the impact of widowhood on friendship to treat the widowed as an homogeneous group. The dominant, though usually implicit, assumption was that this state of itself united people and led to their having essentially similar experiences. While widowhood does structure experience along similar lines, it is also important to be aware that widowhood involves a process through time, rather than just being a steady state. Thus, it is pertinent not just to ask how widowhood affects friendships, or vice versa, but further to enquire about the different forms this relationship takes as widowhood becomes more established.

Elizabeth Bankoff's (1981) insightful analysis of women widowed at a relatively early age highlights the advantages of adopting such a strategy. Her study, which was part of a larger project on widowhood, focuses on the effect friends have on the well-being of women who have been widowed quite recently and who are still experiencing emotional loss. She distinguishes between two groups: first, the 'crisis loss phase' group who had been widowed for eighteen months or less and who were still suffering intense grief; and second, the 'transition phase' group who had been widowed for between two and five years and who were grieving to a more limited extent. By contrasting the impact on her respondents' well-being of three separate categories of friend – widowed and single; married; and neighbourhood based ones – Bankoff is able to show that there are systematic differences in the support required of friends during these two phases of widowhood, and, as a consequence, in the type of friend who can best provide it.

As would be expected, having friends to talk with seemed very important to widows in the 'crisis loss' phase. Expressing their grief and talking through their feelings with their friends was very important for their well-being. Significantly, though, the friends who mattered most in this respect were their still-married friends. At this stage of widowhood, confiding with widowed or neighbourhood friends seemed to have little impact on positive well-being, except that widowed and single friends were important in providing practical guidance and giving comfort when the widows felt especially depressed. As Bankoff argues, because these recently widowed respondents' more established and intimate friendships are likely to be with people who are still married, it will be these friends whom they turn to most for comfort and solace. On the other hand, because many will have experienced equivalent loss, widowed and single friends are likely to be most helpful for coping with the more specific problems of widowhood.

Yet behind this lies another factor, for Bankoff also found that friends' efforts to get widows in the 'crisis loss' phase to adopt a new life style had a negative effect on their well-being (1981). This suggests that, during this phase, the widows had little desire to change their way of life and adapt to the reality of their widowhood. Rather, while still grieving so heavily, they wished to cling to their previous roles and relationships, seeking, in effect, to deny their loss. An important element within this was sustaining their existing friendships and, implicitly or explicitly, rejecting any attempt by their friends to get them to adjust too quickly to their new status.

However, at a later stage, when the pain of bereavement was more muted, they were more able to do this. Thus, as the widows in the 'transition' phase came to cope better with the emotional impact of their husbands' death and grieve less, so they also began to build a new identity for themselves and a more independent life style. In part, this entailed developing new roles and relationships. Certainly, within this the social companionship of friends was important, but, unlike those in the 'crisis loss' phase, their most significant friendships tended to be with other widowed and single people, rather than the still-married. Indeed, generating new friendships instead of relying on their existing married friends generally had a positive impact on these widows' well-being. In other words, stepping out from their previous experience and creating a new self-image at this phase, a process which includes developing new ties of friendship, was beneficial for them.

Bankoff's data was based on a cross-sectional survey, so some of the developmental ideas suggested in her study could not be tested fully, as her carefully considered formulations make evident. Nonetheless, her research is most instructive. Aside from highlighting the need to consider the significance of friendship in terms of the individual's overall social circumstances and environment, it also makes the important point that different friends can be of different consequence at different times. In other words, it counters the tendency there is in much research on friendship to treat the tie as both static and uni-dimensional. As has been emphasised throughout this book, it is important in any analysis of friendship patterns to recognise the processes there are both in the formation and dissolution of different ties and in the character of the dependencies that are generated within them.

CONCLUSION

Most of the studies referred to in this chapter have been small-scale, qualitative ones. They have also been based on samples which were predominantly female and middle-class. Furthermore, many of them are American. As such, their findings can hardly be claimed to be representative of the friendship patterns of Britain's elderly population. Yet while they are limited in scale and in coverage, they remain important, especially within the context of this book, because they illustrate a more adequate approach to the sociological analysis of friendship than is usually found in friendship research. In particular, writers like Jerrome, Adams and Bankoff all focus on the way in which patterns of friendship are shaped by structural factors, rather than simply being a matter of personal choice. Along with the other researchers mentioned, they are also all concerned with the social significance of friendship and the role that it plays in social life.

Obviously many questions still remain. For example, the main studies mentioned do not focus very fully on the economic circumstances of those they study and so say comparatively little about the way in which friendship behaviour is affected by material standing. Indeed, it is noticeable that there has been no recent research equivalent to the above examining the friendships of elderly people with few material resources. It is certainly likely that the friendship patterns of these individuals differ substantially from those of their middle-class contemporaries, given the organisation of working-class friendships at other phases of life and the poverty associated with dependence on state pensions.

Similarly, most research has focused on elderly women, rather than men, reflecting their greater numbers in the population. Relatively little is known specifically about the way in which men's friendship behaviour changes as their circumstances alter with age. What evidence there is, however, appears to be broadly consonant with the themes raised in Chapter 5 (Fischer and Oliker, 1983). In particular, elderly men will continue to have greater access to more public sociable settings in which they can interact with others – at least so long as they remain in sufficiently good health – but are less likely to develop friendships in a form that encourages the disclosure of more intimate or personal feelings. However, a good deal more research is required on the various ways in which the circumstances of ageing affect male friendship patterns before we can get beyond these rather general statements.

While further research is desirable on a number of fronts, this should not detract from the value of the studies discussed in this chapter. They illustrate well some of the main themes this book is attempting to argue. More than the literature on most other aspects of friendship, they take a genuinely sociological stance and show how patterns of friendship are influenced and shaped by the social circumstances of those involved. They focus on their respondents' immediate social environment and examine friend relationships within this broader context. Thus, rather than examining these relationships in the abstract, removed from other aspects of social experience, they are able to indicate the social significance of friendship and the part it plays within the overall patterning of their respondents' lives. Moreover, in the absence of longitudinal research, these studies demonstrate better than most the variation and change that occur in friendship, particularly as people's circumstances alter. They show how both the personnel and the content of friendship can change as previous constraints no longer apply or new ones emerge. In such ways they provide something of a model for the future development of the sociology of friendship.

7

FRIENDSHIP, CRISIS AND CHANGE

This chapter has two related aims. The first is to examine the extent to which people draw on and make use of their friendships in coping with specific problems and contingencies, namely sickness and care provision, domestic violence, unemployment and divorce. The second aim, developing out of this, is to assess the impact of major events in people's lives on the patterns of friendship they maintain. The four issues that form the substantive 'backbone' of the chapter have been selected because they represent a range of quite serious life events in which friends might be expected to become involved. Taken together, they provide a framework for examining the ways in which friends do help each other out and, as important, the ways they do not, both in the shorter and in the longer run.

FRIENDS IN NEED AND FRIENDS IN DEED

According to conventional ideologies, real friends can be relied on to help each other out in times of trouble. Friends are people who can be turned to for assistance and help and who will not worry unduly about the costs involved. As the well-known aphorism asserts, 'A friend in need is a friend indeed'. In other words, friendship is an altruistic relationship, based on an enduring commitment to the other's well-being. Thus, ideally at least, the solidarity that exists between friends is not based solely on sociability and enjoyment, but entails a willingness to provide emotional and practical support as need arises, without heed to self-interest.

It is apparent, however, that not all friendships are drawn on for such support to the same extent. Indeed, this is recognised in common parlance by the distinction which is often made between 'real' and other friendships. As discussed in Chapter 2, 'real' friendships are seen as virtually inalienable. Within them an especially high level of trust has developed, sometimes through one of the sides having previously provided extensive support during some personal crisis. By implication, other friendships cannot be relied on to quite the same degree. The moral commitment that those involved have for one another is less encompassing and less compelling. In practice, they are likely to provide support in many circumstances, but the nature of their relationship means that there will be some limit on the level of support offered and, indeed, accepted.

While suggestive, the distinction commonly made between 'real' and other friendships is, of course, too simplistic, both as a characterisation of relationships and as a predictor of supportiveness. To begin with, the extent to which a particular friend will be used to help cope with a problem will obviously depend in some measure on the nature of the problem faced. Some people will possess useful skills in one area, but not in another. Thus, one friend may be very good at some practical task; another may have more experience or be better suited to deal with personal or emotional problems. Similarly, the extent to which help is provided by friends will be affected by the length of time for which such help is needed. For reasons that will be analysed later, friendships are, in general, better suited to the giving of shorter-term rather than longer-term assistance.

Equally, the degree to which friends are able to provide one another with support will depend on the constellation of their circumstances. While philosophies of friendship emphasise the loyalty friends have for one another, in practice certain other commitments are usually given priority. For example, most people put their family's interests before those of friends, and indeed feel that occupational demands take precedence over those of friendship. Friendship obligations, therefore, are not inevitably paramount. While most will do what they can to help their friends, the benefits of so doing have to be weighed against the costs involved. This, of course, is recognised by those in need of support, who would not expect friends to act in a way that threatens their other, more binding responsibilities. Thus, for example, even close friends are not expected to travel great distances to care for someone during illness. Similarly, there is little expectation that friends should disrupt their own domestic organisation too radically, especially in the long run, in order to meet the needs of a friend. In turn, of course, friends would generally be unhappy to receive such support if it did entail their friend's other commitments suffering. To this extent, friendship is recognised by all as being secondary and having no established claim over resources.

In addition, though, the nature of the actual relationship that friends sustain will influence the type of support exchanged. As already mentioned, the common distinction between 'real' and other friends is too simplistic, but the way in which a relationship is structured will undoubtedly affect the sort of help that will be offered and which it will be considered legitimate to accept. While friendships and other informal ties follow what might be termed 'social guidelines' and are structured in common ways, each tie can also be thought of as developing its own 'rules of relevance' (Paine, 1969; Allan, 1979), which guide the sorts of content considered appropriate to it. To put it another way, as informal relationships develop, they are organised and patterned in particular ways as a result of the circumstances, interests and specific fields of interaction involved. Implicitly, the friends come to share a particular definition of the nature and, importantly, the boundaries of their relationship, with current involvement being premised, albeit flexibly in most cases, around this definition. Inevitably, such definitions change with circumstances, but at any time there is a broad, if tacit, understanding of the character and extent of the solidarity that pertains between them. This understanding plays its part in shaping the types of support which are likely to be offered and accepted by those involved in the relationship.

The rules of relevance can be thought of as operating at two related levels. First, they encompass the situational and contextual boundaries of relationships. As discussed in Chapter 2, some sociable relationships are limited to particular contexts of inter-action – work, a pub, a sports club, etc. The significance of these bounded relationships depends on the overall pattern of sociability which the individuals involved maintain. For some people, they may represent relatively weak ties, with other more significant relation-ships not being so restricted in scope. For others, though, this pattern may be the standard way of organising sociability, so that even the more important of an individual's non-kin relationships tend to be bounded in this way.

Related to this situational framing, though not synonymous with it, is the issue of privacy and the restrictions that are placed on the extent of knowledge that friends have about different aspects of each other's lives. While there is a folk belief that total disclosure is the sign of real friendship, in reality friends rarely know everything about one another. In most friendships, the rules of relevance that develop place limitations on what is revealed. The extent to which sociable relationships are brought into the home is one factor here, as it is harder to limit what is disclosed when interaction routinely occurs in this essentially private sphere. However, just as it is possible to entertain in the home and still maintain a 'front' that restricts knowledge of the self, so, too, it is possible for a good deal of self disclosure to occur and intimate knowledge to develop between people whose interaction is normally bounded by some specific setting.

The point to take from this is that, because of the way in which sociable relationships are framed, not all the problems which an individual encounters are necessarily seen as pertinent to their friendships or as falling within their compass. Perhaps more accurately, even if the nature of the problems is known – as it is likely to be with the sort of more serious occurrences discussed later in this chapter – it does not necessarily follow that systematic support or help in anything but a general sense will be forthcoming or acceptable to those experiencing the problem. There is a strong likelihood that it only will be so if it is congruent with the existing rules of relevance and established boundaries of the relationship. It is important to emphasise that a two-way process is at work here. While some friends may feel it would be inappropriate or too obtrusive for them to interfere in what are defined as private problems, equally, those with the problems may feel it wrong for them to take advantage of their friends or abuse their kind-heartedness, notwithstanding whatever offers those friends may have made. In other words, a similar process occurs to that discussed in the previous chapter, whereby widows sometimes play an active part in their own disengagement from still-married friends for fear of being thought too intrusive.

This indicates a further important issue that influences the extent to which friends and others are drawn into personal difficulties. As well as depending on the nature of the problems faced, the circumstances of the friends and the way their relationship is bounded, the underlying parameters of friendship as a form of personal relationship pattern the support given. Paradoxical though it seems, given the emphasis that altruism receives in conventional accounts of friendship, the exchange basis of the tie often serves to limit the amount of assistance that is provided. The issues of reciprocity and equality, discussed in Chapter 2, lie at the heart of this. The essence of friendship from a sociological standpoint is that it is a tie of equality. This means not just that within the tie there are no hierarchical distinctions, but also that the contributions made by the friends are usually regarded as equivalent. Over time, in other words, there usually needs to be a broad reciprocity to their exchanges if the structural equality of the relationship is to be sustained. Of course, the time span of reciprocation will vary between friendships, as, indeed, will what counts as equivalence. This latter is clearly a subjective matter, with the 'rewards' of relationships often being intangible.

Generally, there are few problems in balancing exchanges with respect to more trivial or short-run assistance, as opportunities to repay such help in one form or another are normally not difficult to find. However, the situation becomes more complicated when the support required is more onerous, time-consuming and long lasting. To begin with, the need for such extensive support often reflects a major change in people's circumstances which may, in any case, make it hard for them to service and sustain their friendships as before. In addition, though, providing long-run assistance is more likely to generate difficulties through interfering with other aspects of the friend's social obligations and life style. Moreover, as we shall see in the cases discussed below, managing friendship often becomes more problematic as the provision of regular, non-reciprocated support by one side may threaten the basis of equality implicit in the relationship. In these circumstances, the majority of friendships are likely to wane. Even if in the long run friends are prepared to offer help, the recipients may feel unhappy about accepting it. They may feel that doing so would place them too much in the debt of the other, without any means of reciprocating and balancing the exchanges.

Given the potential imbalance that can arise in friendships, it is not really surprising that friendship networks tend to undergo change when, for some reason, an individual's situation alters, leaving him or her apparently in need of support for quite lengthy periods. Despite the commitment that friends have towards one another's welfare, in practice the basis of solidarity within the tie does not generally facilitate high levels of long-term unilateral support. Even quite close friendships are liable to dissipate if the circumstances and needs of the individuals are such as to discourage reciprocity and equivalence of exchange. That is to say, the failure of friends to meet what conventionally appears to be the *sine qua non* of genuine friendship is, in fact, the consequence of the way these relationships are normally structured. As we shall see in the examples discussed below, it is not that friends fail to meet their obligations to one another at times of trouble, but more that the organisation of social life makes it difficult for friends to provide support when the circumstances of their lives differ markedly.

SICKNESS AND CARE PROVISION

Most episodes of illness are relatively short events. Despite the growth of medical bureaucracies, the great majority of illness is coped with and catered for within the home, either by the sick individuals themselves or, more frequently, by the household's main domestic carer – usually the wife or mother. While medicines and advice may be obtained from a doctor, routine illness tends to be regarded as a largely private, familial matter with household organisation being sufficiently adaptable to cope with its demands. In recent times, the increased proportion of wives who are employed has made it more difficult for some households to cope with illness than previously, especially when there are dependent children involved. Nevertheless, even where wives are employed, care for those who are ill remains very much a family matter. By and large, the only people from outside the household who are likely to provide substitute care and tending (Parker, 1981) are close female kin – mothers, mothers-in-law, daughters, daughters-in-law and, less frequently, sisters. Of course, the extent to which they are able to provide back-up support will depend not just on their geographical proximity, but also on their own commitments and work obligations.

Overall, it would seem that friends play a rather small part in actively looking after the ill. There is certainly little mention in the research literature of their going into other people's houses to provide care. This, though, does not mean that they are not involved at all in the management of sickness. However, their role is more that of advisor and supporter, either to the sick person or to the principal carer, than that of carer itself. Friends, then, are quite likely to be used as a resource for coping with the care situation, without actually being involved in acts of nursing. Thus, when one of their family is sick, women providing care may discuss the problems they face with their friends. People who feel unwell may turn to their friends for advice over appropriate action, for example whether or not they should go to see a doctor. Other medical matters, too, are frequently discussed with friends, for example, the intricacies of particular forms of treatment or the management of pregnancy (McKinley, 1973; Calnan, 1983; Miles, 1988). In addition, of course, friends may help out in various practical ways, such as doing shopping, collecting medicine or picking children up from school, though the extent to which this happens is likely to be affected by the availability of family support.

Accordingly, friends may be drawn on for support in times of short-term illness, though in the vast majority of cases they are unlikely to be actively involved in the caring role itself, as this is firmly located within the domestic/familial domain. Because the assistance they give tends to be relatively minor, and hence easily reciprocated, accepting such help from friends is usually unproblematic as it does not signify any imbalance or social dependency within the relationship. However, the situation tends to be rather different when the illness is a long-term one. Numerous studies of the chronically ill and handicapped have indicated that friendship plays a very small part in the overall pattern of support and care (Wilkin, 1979; Nissel and Bonnerjea, 1982; Glendinning, 1983; Cecil, Offer and St. Leger, 1987; Qureshi and Simons, 1987). The various reasons for this warrant exploration as they underline the social basis of friendship.

Before doing this, though, it is important to recognise that not all handicapped people require a high degree of tending. Many people with disabilities are quite able to look after themselves and cater for their own personal needs without help from friends or others. The nature of their handicap can still influence their friendship patterns, however. Some may experience few problems in becoming socially integrated; others may find that developing and sustaining friendship ties with able-bodied people is more difficult. For example, the sociable networks of those with chronic conditions that make communication difficult may, through choice or circumstance, be dominated by others similarly afflicted. Gaylene Becker's (1980) fascinating study of the social worlds of deaf people illustrates very well the significance of friendship and the different strategies that people adopt with regard to integration with the non-deaf. In particular, it highlights the reciprocated 'self-help' role of deaf friends in countering stigmatised identities, watching out for one another's welfare, and guarding each other against making potentially embarrassing gaffes in interaction with the non-deaf.

However, as mentioned, friendship appears to play a much smaller part in the lives of those disabled people who need regular, long-term tending. To begin with, these people are likely to have rather few friends. By the nature of their situation, access to the types of social institutions and organisations which provide opportunities for developing and servicing friendships of different forms will be limited. Some, especially those who have been disabled from birth, will have experienced this exclusion throughout their lives. In such cases, it is unlikely that they will have had much chance to generate many friendships. Moreover, given the tendency to social segregation and the emphasis put on status similarity within friendship, a proportion of the friends they do have may be similarly disabled and thus not in a position to provide care.

For others, including the dependent elderly and the long-term sick, the absence of social involvement will represent a change from the past. The consequence, though, is broadly similar. Previous friendships, especially those in which interaction normally occurred in a non-domestic context, are difficult to sustain. Apart from anything else, the fact that the person now ill or infirm can no longer so readily participate in the activities through which the relationship was previously serviced, means that it has to undergo quite a radical change in its basis if it is to continue. In reality, few friendships are able to alter their rules of relevance to this extent, so that in the longer run most tend to become less socially active. In turn, though, their current dependence means they will have few opportunities to make new friendships that can take the place of the old. Thus, in general, the friendship networks of the disabled and the chronically ill tend to be quite restricted, so that any possibility of their friends providing care is small.

Of course, it is not just the friends of those who are ill who might be expected to provide support. The friends of any primary carer there is may also be thought likely to help out where possible. Again, this would seem to be a somewhat romantic view of friendship. An obvious difficulty is that carers often have very little social life of their own, as their time is fully taken up with their caring activities. So, like those they are looking after, they have relatively few opportunities for developing and servicing friendships. Like full-time housewives, only more so, their level of social integration is limited not only by their gender, but also by the privatised, fragmentary and enduring character of their caring tasks. Thus, despite the rhetoric of community care policy, studies of the dependent elderly and of handicapped children have shown consistently that their primary carers lead quite isolated lives (Wilkin, 1979; Nissel and Bonnerjea, 1982; Briggs and Oliver, 1985; Glendinning, 1983).

Besides lacking the external social basis for developing wider social networks, many of these carers, along with other members of the household, may find it difficult to use their home as a setting for sociability with friends because of the apparent dishevelment that caring for a dependent person often creates. Downstairs rooms with beds in them, for example, or the lingering smell of incontinence may be sufficient to discourage any thoughts of inviting others in. Overall, the immediate social environment of many primary carers is, like that of their charges, quite restricted and provides limited possibilities of servicing friendships.

However, even when the chronically infirm or their carers are able to sustain a circle of friends, it is questionable whether these friends would routinely provide much long-term care and support. The problem here lies in the very nature of friendship. To begin with, while friends do care about one another and are concerned for each other's welfare, this is actually quite different from providing practical care. Looking after someone and catering for their needs is simply not the same as, nor necessarily consonant with, the enjoyment and sociability which normally characterises the content of friendship. Such caring represents as much a contradiction as an extension of friendship's underlying principles.

An important factor here is that, in the long run, provision of care by friends almost inevitably generates an imbalance in the relationship by making one individual disproportionately dependent on the other. As argued above, such an imbalance, with one side continually receiving assistance without any acceptable means of reciprocation, is quite contrary to the way in which most friendships are routinely ordered. It entails an exchange basis that fits uneasily into the prevailing rubric of friendship. (There are, of course, some exceptions. Consider, for example, the type of 'patron'-style friendships Robert Edgerton (1967) discusses in his study of mentally-retarded adults. The exchanges in these were by no means reciprocal, though it is also a moot issue whether the 'patrons' involved would characterise the ties as ones of friendship.)

Generally, where there is a pronounced lack of equivalence, the majority of friendships can be expected to fade slowly, notwithstanding the concern and goodwill expressed and genuinely felt within them. In some measure, this will be because the friend who is unable to reciprocate may discourage interaction so as not to make his or her dependence on the other evident. But equally, over time, in most friendships the advantaged friend is likely to find the relationship hard to maintain in the face of the imbalance brought about by their different circumstances. In such ways all but the strongest friendships are likely to become gradually less close and active. (These issues are discussed more fully in Allan, 1986).

Obviously, it is not being suggested here that friends never provide help or care for each other in times of illness. Clearly they do, and this expectaction is built into our notion of friendship. However most are equipped to do so in the short run, especially at times of crisis, rather than the long run. Central to this is the difficulty often experienced in sustaining friendships when the equality and symmetry of the relationship is undermined, as it is when there is a continuing unilateral need for care. Yet some friends will provide practical help over time, despite any resultant imbalance. As noted earlier, these tend to be marked out as 'real' or 'true' friends, with their enduring commitment often being symbolised in kinship terms – 'She's like a sister to me. I can always turn to her.' However, such friendships are not only rare; they are also, as the label implies, qualitatively different from most 'run-of-the-mill', everyday friendships. As a result, it is a mistake to assume they are typical of friendship in general, or that similar patterns of support will be forthcoming from 'ordinary', less committed friendships.

MARITAL VIOLENCE

Since the mid-1970s, there has been increased awareness of the extent to which marital and other forms of domestic violence occur. As yet, though, this awareness has not led to very effective policy initiatives, nor to any significant shift in public attitudes. The tendency is still to 'explain' marital violence in terms of individual pathology – sometimes including in this the victim's own behaviour – rather than by reference to more structural aspects of male domination within marriage. One problem here, of course, is that much domestic violence remains hidden from public view, so that accurate data about it are lacking. Little is known for sure even about the proportion of marriages in which violence occurs, though Marsden (1978) estimates that serious assaults happen in one out of every twenty marriages. The most detailed information about marital violence comes from studies of women living in battered wives' refuges (Dobash and Dobash, 1980; Homer, Leonard and Taylor, 1984; Pahl, 1985). While the experiences of these women may not be totally representative, their accounts provide some evidence of the use made of friends when violence occurs and the types of support they give. In the process, they illustrate the boundaries that are usually drawn around friendships and the influence of external factors on them.

It is worth stressing that not all women experiencing marital violence have friends – or anyone else – to turn to for support. In Pahl's study, for example, ten of the forty-two women she interviewed had no friend or relative from whom they felt they could get help, while a further twelve had only one such person (Pahl, 1985). In part, this is a consequence of kinship ties breaking down through the impact of divorce, death and geographical mobility. A combination of other processes can operate to limit involvement with friends, some of which are more subtle than others. Thus, some violent husbands actively restrict their wives' social contact by 'policing' their movements and threatening them with further violence if they talk to outsiders (Homer, Leonard and Taylor, 1985). In extreme cases this can involve effectively imprisoning wives within their own homes. Equally, some wives themselves withdraw from social contact because of the shame and embarrassment they feel about their situation. For those who are full-time housewives such isolation is, of course, not difficult to establish. In turn, some women become isolated because existing friends gradually distance themselves, rather than get embroiled in domestic conflict.

However, even if the women involved do have a circle of friends, this does not necessarily mean they will turn to them for support after being abused. Interestingly, in the Dobashs' research, the pattern tended to be for their respondents either to develop closer and stronger bonds with particular friends in whom they had confided their problems, or else to isolate themselves and avoid contact with friends as much as possible (Dobash and Dobash, 1980). The reasons for not confiding in friends, where they exist, are complex. As noted above, some husbands will deliberately restrict the opportunities their wives have for discussing their problems by controlling and monitoring their movements. In other cases the reasons have more to do with the image that the women have of domestic violence and the shame they feel about it happening to them.

To begin with, the violence is quite often defined as a private matter, like other domestic arguments and tiffs. The ideology of the privatised family is important here, for there is a strong belief that what goes on in the home, especially if it reflects badly, should not be broadcast outside. In some cases, the wife may want to protect her husband from public censure, particularly if she sees the violence as an isolated (and perhaps even excusable) event, rather than as a continuing feature of her marriage. More frequently, there is the feeling that she is in some way to blame for the violence, or at least that others will see it in this light. As Dobash and Dobash remark, the sense of shame and stigma so commonly experienced by battered wives is closely related to 'our cultural ideals about the nature of a good marriage and about the woman's responsibility for ensuring that the marital relationship is successful' (Dobash and Dobash, 1980, p.166).

One further factor that discourages confiding in friends or other outsiders is a belief that they are not really in a position to understand. In the main, abused wives tend to feel isolated in their experience; others are thought to have no knowledge of it and, therefore, are thought not to be in a position to provide help or support. This sense of isolation can build on popular stereotypes and reinforce feelings of guilt and shame: because an abused wife's problem is so abnormal she must be partly to blame for the abuse she receives and thus bear some responsibility for her predicament (Homer *et al.*, 1985).

As the Dobashs argue, such concerns become less crucial as women's experience of violence continues. At later stages, they are more likely both to turn to informal contacts for help and to seek assistance from formal agencies (Dobash and Dobash, 1984). Though the research evidence is somewhat limited, it would appear that some half to three-quarters of abused wives do approach friends for support at some stage during their violent marriage. For example, in Pahl's study, two-thirds of the sample had discussed their problems with at least one friend (1985, p,80), while in the Dobashs' research, 53 of the 109 respondents had done so (Dobash, Dobash and Cavanagh, 1985, p.148). In the Middlesbrough study 57 of the 80 women interviewed had approached either friends or neighbours for help (Homer *et al.*, 1985, p.105). Thus, for some abused women, friends do act as a resource, though somewhat less so than relatives, especially parents, do. However it needs to be emphasised that friends as a category are not turned to for support by abused women to any major extent. There is certainly no evidence that they involve a wide circle of friends in their problems. Rather, domestic violence appears largely to lie outside the purlieu of friendship, with the stigma associated with it being such that most women try to conceal their experiences from most of their friends and other sociable contacts. This reflects the pattern in which most friendships are organised. Routine friendship as a form of social relationship may or may not involve interaction in the home; it may or may not involve the married couple as a unit. Either way, it does not normally entail direct intervention in, nor even intimate knowledge of, domestic relations, which are seen as private and as essentially outside the realm of all but the closest friendships. This applies particularly to more serious manifestations of domestic conflict, even though such conflict may give rise to concern. Indeed, for some this concern may, perversely, discourage full revelation of their situation, as people may not want to put themselves in the position of being pitied by their friends. This, too, would contravene the implicit rules around which most friendships are built.

In similar fashion, when friends are confided in, the forms of support they are likely to provide are constrained by the rules of friendship and, not least, by the acceptance that the demands of friendship should not for long interfere with the friend's day-to-day life, nor prevail over that person's other commitments, especially domestic and familial ones. Thus, when the type of assistance given to abused women by their friends is examined it is, in fact, quite limited. As Dobash and Dobash (1980) point out, the vast majority of approaches that abused women make to third parties are for either moral support or accommodation. In general, the friends approached by abused women do appear to be very supportive and willing to spend a lot of time listening to and talking through their problems. The value of this should not be underestimated, especially given the isolation that abused women often feel and the trepidation with which they first broach the issue. Nonetheless, talking about problems, of itself, does not alter the women's situation, nor stop the violence.

Friends, however, are rarely in a position to do a great deal more than listen and offer advice. Occasionally they may be able to give more active support, for instance, going with the abused women to see a doctor, social worker or solicitor, or caring for children for a short while (Dobash and Dobash, 1980). Generally, though, their role is quite limited; their main service is just that of being a sympathetic listener. Thus, they are unlikely to provide the abused women with alternative accommodation for anything but an immediate crisis. Nor are they likely to intervene directly in the marital relationship. As emphasised above, at the heart of this are not just the facilities or expertise that friends have, but more the construction of friendship as a form of relationship and its position within the hierarchy of social obligation.

It is not just while violence is occurring that friends can be supportive. Friends are also often an important resource to women who have decided to leave their husbands and set up a new home. In some instances, it will be established friends who are most helpful at such times. The research on women's refuges, though, also emphasises the significance of new friendships and contacts made in the hostel with other women who have experienced similar problems. Again, what is important here is simply having people to talk to who, because of their own background, understand the difficulties faced and the feelings aroused. With these friends, questions of shame or pity do not disturb the balance of equality in the relationship, as each side shares the same identity. On top of this, though, friends who have already had to face the difficulties of setting up home and coping with the dilemmas of single parenthood are able to provide a good deal of practical support, advice and reassurance at a time when confidence is usually rather low. Whether known previously, or first met at the refuge or since leaving, such friends often act as a central resource in meeting the new pressures and demands that abused women face when they make the break from their husbands. (Pahl, 1985; Binney, Harkell and Nixon, 1985). The significance of friendships between people who share the experience of marital breakdown will be developed further in the section below on divorce and friendship.

UNEMPLOYMENT AND FRIENDSHIP

With the numbers of unemployed people growing to well over three million in the 1980s and affecting more than ten per cent of the workforce, unemployment has been the focus of much popular and academic comment. As McKee and Bell (1986) point out, most discussions of unemployment tend to focus on an economic model of man in which his role as an ex-worker is paramount. Understanding the economics of unemployment is, of course, important, as is an appreciation of the way in which changes in the labour market affect opportunities for secure re-employment. Certainly, despite continued speculation about the existence of 'welfare scroungers' and 'black economies', there is no room to doubt that unemployment quickly leads the majority of people into poverty (Marsden and Duff, 1975; Clark, 1978; Sinfield, 1981; McKee, 1987). However, the dominance of the 'economic model of man' has encouraged a rather narrow perspective on the effects of unemployment. Thus, with a few notable exceptions (Coyle, 1984; Cragg and Dawson, 1984; Martin and Wallace, 1984), not only do most studies ignore female unemployment (Marshall, 1984), but so, too, they tend to disregard its impact on the domestic, familial and other social relationships of those affected. In most cases, of course, this includes not just the unemployed, but also the others living in his or her household.

It is now well recognised that, apart from poverty, one of the main consequences of continuing male unemployment is social isolation and a reduction of involvement in many of the social contexts in which much male sociability routinely occurs. Obviously important in this is the loss of opportunity to engage in the work-based relationships which are built into most types of employment. Whether or not they are explicitly recognised as friendships, ties with workmates and colleagues provide an important mechanism of social integration, however much they tend to be taken for granted in practice.

But it is not just the absence of work contacts that can lead to a reduction in sociable involvement. The poverty associated with unemployment is also important, as many forms of sociability require some financial expenditure. For example, socialising in pubs and social clubs or participating in sports activities may be ruled out for many unemployed people because of the costs involved. In a similar way, established patterns of activity in existing friendships may no longer be viable. The costs of going out with friends, or even of entertaining them at home, may prove prohibitive on reduced income (Wallace, 1987). Furthermore, the stigma of unemployment may also discourage sociable activities, especially with those who are still in employment. As an example, Brah (1986) reports that one of her respondents had virtually stopped attending family and community gatherings to avoid being asked questions about his unemployment.

As noted above, the isolating effects of unemployment have, in most studies, been seen from the perspective of the unemployed male. Nonetheless, the evidence there is indicates equally clearly that unemployed females also experience social isolation and a reduction in friendships, not least when unemployment entails their being re-cast into a dependent housewife role (Coyle, 1984; Cragg and Dawson, 1984; Martin and Wallace, 1984). It is also important to recognise that male unemployment often has a marked impact on other household members, and, in particular, on wives. As McKee and Bell (1986) demonstrate, not only does a husband's unemployment affect the material conditions of family life and make the task of managing the household's economy more difficult, but the wife's own social space becomes more restricted. Principally because of the ways in which the state benefit system operates, wives of unemployed men are far less likely to be employed themselves, especially if their husbands' unemployment is long-term. Together with the household's lack of resources, this of itself tends to limit a wife's opportunities for social involvement with friends and others. But, in addition, her husband's increased presence in the home may further discourage any sociable activities on her part. In McKee and Bell's terms (1986), she may become 'doubly isolated' because his presence alters the use made of domestic space, either directly through the control he exerts over her activities or indirectly through others not wanting to interfere in what they take to be the couple's domestic privacy.

In such ways the social involvement and friendship networks of the unemployed and their families can become quite limited. Patently, though, unemployment does not affect everyone who experiences it in the same way. To some degree, each individual's experience will be patterned by their structural location and by situational circumstances. For example, unemployment will affect older workers in different ways from younger ones; the problems faced by couples with dependent children will be different from those faced by people without such commitments; there will be differences between households experiencing multiple unemployment and households in which, say, a school leaver is without a job. Similarly, in the longer run, the maintenance or otherwise of friendship networks will be influenced by the employment experiences of the others known. It may, for instance, prove easier to maintain friendships when others in one's network are also out of work than when most are employed.

Binns and Mars (1984) recognise this potential for diversity in their study of fifty households in 'The Heights', a Glasgow housing estate with an unemployment rate of thirty per cent. Amongst other issues, they show how unemployment tended to have different consequences for couples in which the male was aged under twenty-five than for those in which he was older than this. Unlike the latter, the younger respondents had little or no experience of employment, having been mostly unemployed since leaving school. In the main, they had also been brought up in 'The Heights', so through school and the neighbourhood had established quite developed local networks of friends and peers. Whereas the social experiences of the older group of respondents generally mirrored that outlined above – most withdrawing 'into the increasingly non-supportive world of nuclear home and hearth' (Binns and Mars, 1984, pp.677–8) – the younger group's responses were somewhat different. A minority of these younger men spent much of their time with other unemployed men. The majority, however, had shifted their 'social centre of gravity' (Binns and Mars, 1984, p.691) to their home and family, though without becoming isolated to the extent the older respondents were.

Because most of these younger respondents had never experienced extensive or secure employment, their domestic and social lives had been constructed within the context of unemployment and poverty. As a consequence, unemployment had not led to a loss of income, nor had it altered their patterns of sociability and friendship. All but four of the twenty-five younger men had lived in 'The Heights' as children, and thus were well integrated with others who, because of the high levels of youth unemployment in the area, were in a similar position to themselves. Although money was certainly scarce, they and their wives were able to maintain friendships with others, either in couple relationships or individually. As would be expected, the men appeared to have greater freedom and space for this than their wives who, as in McKee and Bell's (1986) study, continued to bear primary responsibility for child care and other domestic tasks. The men, in particular, benefited from the local authority's policies of subsidising the cost of leisure and sporting facilities for the unemployed. For many of them, activities like golf, bowling and football provided a convenient focus for sociability and meeting with friends.

Aside from issues of social participation, friends may be influential in helping unemployed people find employment or other types of economic activity, as Morris's (1984) research in Port Talbot demonstrates. In particular, those in employment may be able to alert unemployed friends about forthcoming vacancies before these are advertised more widely. Such informal mechanisms for recruitment are popular with some employers, partly because they save costs but also because the use of personal contact fosters greater loyalty and commitment (Jenkins *et al.*, 1983). With the recession and the growth in short-term contract work, these recruitment strategies have become increasingly significant, not least when the job is 'off the cards' or in some other way contravenes employment law. However, as with the impact of unemployment on social participation, the degree to which an individual's friendship circle can be effective in helping him or her to find a new job will vary.

On the surface, the unemployed with the greatest chance of obtaining work would appear to be those with the most extensive contacts with people employed in different organisations and industries. While this is generally true, in areas of high unemployment the quality of the relationships will also matter. It is not enough, in other words, just to know people with job information; it is also important that they tell you about the work before they tell any of their other contacts. Thus, where there is competition, Granovetter's (1973) arguments about the structural significance for information flow of 'weak ties' in social networks would seem questionable. Instead, as Morris's (1984) research indicates, those most likely to hear about job vacancies are those who maintain relatively close friendships with a wide group of others. As has been argued, though, many unemployed people find this quite difficult to do, mainly because they lack the necessary resources to sustain extensive friendship circles.

In Morris's study, the people who were most likely to obtain work, albeit often short-term and unpleasant, through informal channels were those who had a 'collective' pattern of sociability. They tended, in other words, to be the ones who through active membership of a rugby club or other such organisation managed, despite their unemployment, to sustain a strong sense of group solidarity and identity. In contrast, those with a small number of dyadic, dispersed friendships – Morris's 'individualistic' pattern – were less likely to hear of jobs informally and spent longer periods without employment, though when they did obtain work it tended to be more secure (Morris, 1984). While some questions remain from Morris's research – for example, how important is collective solidarity *vis-à-vis* the extent of close ties, and for how long can such patterns be maintained with limited resources? – it raises interesting issues about the role of friendship in the lives of the unemployed.

DIVORCE AND FRIENDSHIP

The majority of people who experience marital breakdown find it traumatic and difficult to handle. In consequence, one might expect people to need their friends at this time and turn to them for support and help. Similarly, in theory, friends could play a significant role in helping those who have been through a divorce to reconstruct their lives and overcome the difficulties they now face. While there have been few longitudinal studies of network change following divorce (Leslie and Grady, 1985), the research there has been suggests that in practice the role of friends is less clear-cut. Certainly, existing friends appear generally supportive at the time of the separation. However, in the longer run there tends to be at least a partial 'transformation in the nature and extent of relationships linking the individual to others in his social universe' (Hart, 1976, p.159). Those who do not quickly remarry, or otherwise form a new couple, often find that the opportunities they have for sociable participation are curtailed. Rather than being supported or cocooned by their existing ties, many instead come to feel quite marginal and excluded and find they need to develop new friendships (Spanier and Casto, 1979; Milardo, 1987).

Like marital breakdown itself, changes in the friendship circles of the divorced do not arise suddenly. Instead, they are one element in the drawn-out process by which an individual's status position and self-identity slowly alter. As argued earlier, friendship in its generic form is as much about enjoyment and sociability as it is about confiding and giving support. In consequence, while some friends may be turned to, especially by females, as domestic conflict becomes more serious, in other cases the conflict will undermine the friendship and result in reduced involvement, just as it does in cases of domestic violence. This is particularly likely to be so with couple-based friendships, as the marital tension will make interaction less relaxed and pleasurable. Either the friends will find the situation uncomfortable and too difficult to handle, or else the couple themselves will tend to withdraw from them in order to avoid publicising their difficulties. Thus, even before any separation or divorce, there is a tendency for those involved to become more isolated, reduce their contact with existing friends and so not really be in a position to turn to them for support.

There is likely to be even greater disruption of friendship networks after divorce. The extent of it depends not just on the nature of the friendships existing beforehand, but also on the changes that occur in the individual's circumstances afterwards. As numerous studies have shown, separation and divorce frequently result in quite radical changes in people's material situation, especially when there are dependent children involved (Marsden, 1969; Finer, 1974; Popay, Rimmer and Rossiter, 1983). These changes, in turn, can have a major impact on the friendships and sociable ties maintained. To begin with, separation and divorce may lead to loss of income and a reduction in living standards, with few resources being left for sociability. Female-headed single parent families are particularly likely to be in poverty, with some seventy-five per cent being on or near to Income Support levels (Popay *et al.*, 1983). Others may not be in poverty as such, but still find that their income is no longer sufficient to maintain their established patterns of social activity.

Apart from reduced living standards, divorce also quite often results in geographical mobility for one or both spouses. This may be through choice – so as to make a fresh start – or because the previous accommodation can no longer be afforded. Such mobility is itself likely to disrupt people's patterns of sociability and make the servicing of existing friendships that much more difficult. As many divorcees know to their cost, replacing these ties and developing new contacts is not always easy, especially, perhaps, for those females whose leisure participation is constrained by child care responsibilities as well as by social convention (Milardo, 1987). Furthermore, when people are mobile following separation or divorce, it quite often involves a move to less satisfactory housing than they lived in before. In more extreme cases – for example, if they move back with parents or into lodgings – this can hinder the development of new sociable ties, as well as the maintenance of old ones, by making home-based sociable activity difficult.

In part, the extent to which friendships change with separation and divorce depends on the degree to which those involved alter their social activities as a result of the marital break-up. As noted, where previously activities have been couple-based, friendship patterns are likely to be affected quite markedly (Marsden, 1969; Spanier and Casto, 1979; Milardo, 1987). On the other hand, where the couple have tended to socialise separately, then the divorce may have rather less impact, especially if the activities engaged in tend to be confined to specific contexts. In other words, assuming financial and other material circumstances allow, those relationships which are embedded in non-domestic social organisation are less likely to be affected by marital disruption than those which are more broadly based or involve sociability in the home. With the former, 'mate'-type relationships, the individual's domestic circumstances, and any alteration to them, are usually less salient than in the latter. As was evident in the discussion of widowhood in the previous chapter, there are numerous reasons why couple-based friendships gradually tend to dissipate after marital separation. For a number of less close ones, the absence of the couple as a sociable unit is itself the reason for their decline. Similarly, where the interaction and friendship had been dependent mainly on the ex-spouse's activities and social position, then again it is likely to fade once the couple separate. In other cases, more subtle processes operate. For example, the nature of the friendship almost certainly alters when, instead of two couples interacting, it is one couple and a single individual. The balance and equivalence of the tie is undermined, with the old activities no longer being so viable or easily managed. Buying rounds of drinks, playing cards, conversations between pairs, exchanging meals, and the like all become that much more difficult and tend to form a wedge between the friends. What was previously effortless because of their equivalent status now becomes more of a problem, just as it does for widows. But in addition to these processes, the divorcee may also slowly withdraw from the friendship (Spanier and Casto, 1979; Milardo, 1987). This may be for financial reasons, but it can also be because the 'problem' of the divorce tends to change the focus of the friendship. Apart from the types of strain just discussed, some of those experiencing divorce fear or resent what they see as friends' interference in their lives and withdraw from these relationships to avoid it. Thus in Hart's (1976) study, a number of her respondents recognised that they had cut themselves off from some of their previous friends because they did not want to change the basis of the relationship they had had and put themselves in the position of receiving sympathy or pity.

The social opprobrium of divorce has certainly lessened over the last generation, as the numbers directly or indirectly involved have increased (Allan, 1985). Nonetheless, many of those going through marital separation and divorce still feel stigmatised. Aside from a sense of failure and shame, the reaction of friends and other acquaintances is important here. To begin with, people are well aware that once their marital problems are made public, those in their social network will, maliciously or otherwise, gossip and talk about their situation. Similarly, however well-intentioned, the supportive reactions of friends can effectively mark out the differences that now exist, especially after any immediate crisis is over. Equally, the gradual distancing from previous friendships also indicates the changed status of the divorced and, along with the other changes that have occurred, can result in a strong sense of being stigmatised. This, in turn, or the fear of it, can in some ways feed on itself through the divorced not putting themselves in potentially embarrassing situations, instead shying away from involvement in their previous relationships.

For such reasons as these the friendship circles of the separated and divorced are likely to alter. As elsewhere, though, gender plays its part. Although there are few studies which deliberately contrast the experience of males and females in this respect, it would seem that these processes are likely to leave males less socially disadvantaged than females (Milardo, 1987). To begin with, after divorce, men are likely to be financially better off than many women, principally because of the gender biases of the labour market and the limited amount of maintenance most pay (Maclean and Eekelaar, 1983). Equally, women are more likely to be constrained by child care and the limits this places on sociable activities. In addition, though, following from the discussion in previous chapters, men tend to have more access to public and other leisure facilities and associations. Together with their employment, this generally means that they can more easily maintain sociable contacts following divorce or substitute new ties for ones that have lapsed (Milardo, 1987; O'Brien, 1987). Further, men are more likely to be involved in 'mate'-type relationships from which domestic issues tend to be excluded, so that their divorce is likely to have less impact.

In contrast, family and domestic matters are so central to most married women's social position that the issue of their separation and divorce is far less likely to be excluded from even their more restricted friendships. Thus, while, in line with the discussion in Chapter 5, women undergoing divorce may have more friends with whom they can confide and discuss their problems, overall it would seem probable that divorce has less impact on male friendship patterns. American research suggests that women, particularly those caring for young children, tend to become more dependent on primary kin relationships for companionship and support in the period following divorce, a feature which is likely to be the case in Britain as well (Milardo, 1987).

Generally, then, the friendship networks of the divorced undergo significant changes when their marriages end. Of course, some change would have occurred in any case over time, as friendship circles are rarely static. However, the changes that occur with separation and divorce do usually seem to be more radical. In particular, for those who remain unattached, the likelihood is that a high proportion of their friendships will be with others in a similar position. As the friendships they had when they were married gradually wane – as we have seen, not through explicit rejection, but through more subtle processes which reflect the lack of balance now existing in the previous ties – they will tend to be replaced by other separated and divorced people (Rands, 1988). With them there is no imbalance, for they are more likely to share a similar social and economic position as well as the experience of marital breakdown. They can, consequently, provide support without its appearing to be patronising and sociability without any sense of difference or lack of fit (Marsden, 1969; Hart, 1976). While friendships do change like this, the process is not straightforward and can often be painful. As mentioned earlier, isolation and loneliness are continuing problems for many divorcees. The problem, as Chester (1977) points out, is that despite high levels of divorce, as yet no effective mechanisms have been found for reintegrating those involved into what is still essentially a couple-dominated society – aside, of course, from remarriage or a less formal union.

DISCUSSION

While the examples which have been used in this chapter to illustrate the role of friendship in times of trouble or change differ quite markedly from one another, there are, nonetheless, a number of common features that stand out. Five issues in particular will be raised briefly here, though, of course, it must always be recognised that the behaviour of friends in particular circumstances is not going to be uniform. The ways in which different people react to the predicaments they or their friends find themselves in undoubtedly vary, so that the points which follow need to be recognised as generalisations which do not necessarily always apply.

The first point to make is an obvious one: friends do provide one another with help and support in times of trouble or crisis. They do act as a resource which people generally use to help them deal with the difficulties they face. The support they give may be practical or emotional or both. Thus, it can range from, say, helping to manage illness through to providing a sounding board for talking about marital difficulties and dilemmas. Yet, as is clear from the studies cited above, not all friends are used as resources in this way to the same degree. Apart from some friends being closer and more involved in personal matters than others, which friend is turned to often depends on the situation in hand and previous experience. However, the fact that some friends are not really confided in or turned to for help does not necessarily imply any failure on their part. Often it would seem that people attempt to cope on their own and hide or disguise the problems they are facing in order not to involve their friends. At times this is because they feel a sense of shame about their situation and do not want to make it public. At other times, a sense of shame may not be paramount, but, nonetheless, they may not wish to be seen as a burden on their friends, or to be pitied or stigmatised in some other well-meaning way.

Secondly, it is apparent that the support which friends normally give – and are normally expected to give – tends to be short-term or medium-term, rather than long-term. Long-term assistance occasionally occurs, but appears not to be common. As a problem continues, the part that friends in general play in coping with it gradually declines. Those who start off offering advice or providing practical help are likely to withdraw slowly. An obvious example is the way in which friends may help people cope with acute illness but will be less involved with chronic conditions. Here it needs to be remembered that while friends are committed to one another at a personal level and while our concept of friendship does entail some obligation to offer support, a dominant theme in most friendships is that they are about sociability and enjoyment, rather than service and longer-term help. This, together with the recognition that friends have a lesser call on people's resources than other ties like family or employment, is a major factor in people's unwillingness to ask for or accept extensive help from friends or become too indebted to them.

The third point to emphasise is closely tied in with this. It is that friendship circles are dynamic, rather than static. An individual's friendships alter and change over time. This occurs anyway over the life course, but becomes particularly apparent at times of prolonged crisis or major change. Thus, as argued above, people whose marriages end, who become chronically infirm or who experience some other long-term change in their circumstances are likely to find that their friendship circles alter in response. They gradually become less involved with those who at one time were quite central in their patterns of sociability. In many cases, others are found to replace these friends, though in some situations high levels of social isolation may result. As discussed earlier in this chapter, once the social position of those who are friends differs significantly, maintaining their friendship often becomes problematic. Without again going through the different factors involved in this, the portrayal of the relationship as one between equals becomes less taken-for-granted and less easy as the situation of the friends diverges.

Fourthly, as implied above, some crises are seen as having moral overtones more than others. In such cases, people are likely to try to disguise or underplay the problems they are experiencing and be reticent about involving their friends in them. For example, whatever the reality, the belief that people – and perhaps especially women – are in some sense responsible for the conduct of their marriage often means that some of those faced with major marital difficulties tend not to confide in their friends. They may instead either pretend that there are no problems or else withdraw from contact with friends, rather than be faced with constant questions, attention and concern. Besides a desire to maintain an acceptable self image with their friends, this reflects the significance of sustaining equality and structural balance within friendships. Moreover, it highlights the importance of seing the waning of friendship in times of crisis as a two-way process. It is not simply a matter of friends rejecting or ignoring people with problems, but a more complex process, whereby those apparently in need of support tend to distance themselves and withdraw from contact with their friends. It seems likely that other forms of 'deviance' will have a similar impact on friendships, though there appears to have been little research specifically examining this.

The final issue to emphasise here concerns the role of 'real friends' in periods of crisis and change. As mentioned in earlier parts of the book, a distinction is often made between friends in general and 'real friends'. Typically, these are people either with whom friendship has been maintained over a long time, despite various changes of circumstances, or else people who have provided high levels of support and 'stood by' the individual at times of personal crisis. Such friendships are quite different from most friendships, but in turn they cannot be seen as providing an appropriate model for friendship generally. Their significance arises from the fact that they are exceptional. Equally, though, it should be recognised that such friendships do not necessarily develop from what previously were the most significant friendships that an individual maintained. As raised in the discussion of marital violence, those who 'stand by' the individual and provide the support that sees him or her through a crisis may be people previously unknown, or only known vaguely. In such cases, the rapport that develops between them often seems to be based on their having shared the crisis experience, rather than on a personal commitment arising from more routine sociability. To conclude, this again suggests that the majority of existing, 'run-of-the-mill' friendships may not be organised or 'framed' in a manner that renders them inherently suitable for providing extensive support at times of major personal crisis. To assume they are is to misunderstand their social basis.

8

FRIENDSHIP, SOCIABILITY
AND SOCIAL STRUCTURE

The central argument of this book has been that friendship patterns are not solely a matter of individual discretion or choice, but that they are influenced by a range of structural factors which, to some degree, lie outside the control of the individual. The aim of this chapter is to complement earlier ones by developing further some of the themes which they contain. In particular, the intention is to discuss how different forms of sociability arise from different social conditions. That is, while the broader, more societally oriented questions posed in Chapter 1 will not all be addressed, the focus will be on the way in which the organisation of friendship ties within various sections of the population is related to their different social and material experiences. In this, the chapter will be especially concerned with some of the issues raised in Chapters 2, 3 and 4.

The starting point for this discussion is the distinction made in Chapter 2 between those forms of friendship which are routinely bound to particular contexts and those which are more open-ended and permit interaction in a range of settings. On the basis of previous research (Allan, 1977a; 1979), it was there argued that members of the middle class tend to adopt the more open form and use involvement in different settings, including the home, as a way of developing and demonstrating the strength of their friendships. In contrast, it was suggested that members of the working class less frequently develop friendships in this manner, but instead often restrict the boundaries of even their more significant informal relationships to specific social arenas.

In his cogent appraisal of these arguments, R. G. A. Williams (1983) has suggested that the relationship between patterns of sociability and class is rather more complex than this dichotomy implies. Certainly, the categorisation of the population into two broad groupings on the basis of (male) manual or non-manual employment is too broad and too mechanical a division. Williams's critique, however, goes beyond this. In effect, he argues that the form which friendship typically takes is unlikely to depend on type of employment alone. Instead what is necessary in order to understand the generation of different forms of sociability is a rather wider view of class. Thus, as well as employment, factors such as housing, geographical mobility and community organisation are also important in shaping the typical forms that sociability takes. So while Williams accepts that sociability in traditional working-class localities tends to be contextually framed, he suggests this will be far less the case amongst other working-class households, such as those purchasing their homes on newly-built estates, where similar social and economic conditions are not found.

The importance of Williams's work lies not so much in its empirical criticism as in the insight it gives to the mechanisms by which different forms of sociability emerge. In order to see this and develop the arguments made earlier in this book, it is helpful to examine the factors influencing sociability in traditional working-class localities and contrast these with those patterning the form that friendship typically takes amongst the established middle class. From this base it will be possible to develop the analysis more generally.

TRADITIONAL WORKING-CLASS COMMUNITIES

During the 1950s and 1960s urban, community and family sociologists devoted a good deal of effort to analysing the social organisation of what are generally described as traditional working-class communities. In the main, these were inner-city localities, such as Bethnal Green in London (Young and Willmott, 1957), St. Ebbe's in Oxford (Mogey, 1956) and St. Ann's in Nottingham (Coates and Silburn, 1970), which were characterised by inadequate housing and a declining economic base. As a consequence of industrial development and relocation, together with post-war attempts to improve the housing stock through slum clearance, many of these areas were in a state of decline and would apparently soon disappear altogether, at least in their current form. Given the general climate of social and economic renewal, sociologists were, not surprisingly, interested in charting the contours of social organisation within these communities and assessing the impact that the new affluence would have on the lives of their residents. Many, like Mogey (1956) and Young and Willmott (1957), were explicitly concerned with analysing the changes that arose as people were rehoused on new estates.

Thus, at the time of the studies, these localities were clearly experiencing a major period of transition. Their traditional industries were declining. So, too, their populations were decreasing as the new housing policies took effect. Yet, at the same time, there appeared to be a stability and constancy in these localities, as the dominant life styles found within them seemed to represent a continuation of the traditional patterns established by previous generations. While, as always, such an account underestimates previous levels of change, the social characteristics of the surviving populations tended to encourage this view (Cornwell, 1984).

Demographically, the most notable feature of the localities was the pattern of mobility occurring within them. While many people were leaving the areas, either for reasons of employment or new housing, very few were moving into them. In consequence, those that remained not only shared a similar disadvantaged class position, but a high proportion had spent their entire lives in or near to these localities. Thus, the populations of these traditional communities tended to be remarkably homogeneous. Most belonged to the lower working class, involved in semi-skilled or unskilled work. Most had inadequate, privately rented housing, frequently sharing basic amenities like toilet and water systems, and sometimes even cooking facilities, with neighbours. Most also had extensive social networks in the locality, based on long-term residence, overlapping ties of kinship and neighbouring, and common involvement in a range of local institutions, including schools. As a result, there tended to be strong feelings of identification with the localities and wide-ranging knowledge about the circumstances of quite large numbers of others living within them.

A close reading of the various empirical studies of this form of traditional working-class community reveals marked similarities in the patterns of sociability and friendship that occurred in them. Essentially, the dominant form that friendship took in these localities was that of mateship. In other words, notwithstanding the extensive local networks in which people were involved and the sense of community this generated, most non-kin sociable relationships tended to be framed by specific activities and settings, rather than being more free-floating and independent of context in the way that middle-class friendships typically are. Thus, little effort was made to develop sociable relationships by involving individuals in a range of different settings or pastimes. Instead, even the more significant non-kin relationships an individual sustained were, to this degree, limited in their scope. Furthermore, interaction was often perceived as arising haphazardly, rather than through deliberate co-ordination. So, for example, even when time was regularly spent with the same people in some activity, the rationale for the interaction tended to be expressed in terms of that given activity, rather than for the overt purpose of meeting these others. One went to the pub – or whatever – for a drink and not specifically to see A or B, although they would almost certainly be there.

This organisation of sociability can be recognised as being framed around three related dichotomies or oppositions, with the boundary in each being quite rigidly delineated. First, a clear distinction was made between public and private spheres of activity or, more specifically, between the home and outside activities. Outside the home there was a broad expectation of communal involvement and gregariousness. In this, relationships were rightly characterised by friendliness and warmth. Yet such relationships were largely restricted to the public sphere. Ties that developed there were not carried over into the home, which remained an essentially private shield not open to the public gaze.

This was closely related to the second characteristic distinction: that between family, in a general sense, and non-family. Family, a category which in this context could include quite a range of kin, formed something of a moral unit. Unlike non-family, they could be party to domestic routines and be trusted not to spread unwanted gossip. Non-family, on the other hand, even when they had been known for some considerable length of time, tended to be excluded from the home. With the exception of emergencies, they were generally only invited in on special occasions and then entertained in a quite formal, almost ritualistic fashion.

The third dichotomy of significance here was that betweeen males and females. Within these traditional communities male and female activities and leisure pursuits were normally strongly demarcated. There was little overlap between them, outside the courting phase of early adulthood, or consequently in the sets of informal friendships in which they were involved. Outside kinship, each was principally incorporated into a single gender sociable network. As we shall see, the importance of these dichotomies is that they illustrate the way in which patterns of friendship are integrated with broader aspects of social and economic life.

As already mentioned in Chapter 2, a major reason why sociable relationships tended to be restricted to specific contexts outside the home stemmed from the material conditions of life in these localities. Two aspects of this are worth mentioning. First, the circumstances of the home and of domestic life were anything but luxurious. Most households tended to be overcrowded and to have few amenities. While many were 'homely' in the traditional sense, they did not necessarily provide an ambience that was conducive to entertaining. Similarly, there were not always the resources available to meet the costs that entertaining routinely involves. Secondly, structuring relationships around particular social contexts and events quite effectively limits the demands that can be made of you. While, clearly, within any social context obligations arise entailing reciprocity and therefore expense, these can be managed more readily when they are restricted to specific settings. If nothing else, by determining the extent to which they are involved in the setting, each individual retains control over the costs that such sociability entails in a way which may prove more difficult when the basis of the relationship is broader.

But, in addition to control over the financial costs of sociability, these patterns also allow a readier control of information than when friendship is less context-specific. In particular, the exclusion of non-kin from the home ensures that a greater wall of privacy can be constructed around the domestic sphere than is otherwise the case. As Williams (1983) notes, exercising such control was especially necessary, given the structural characteristics of the working-class communities in question. Not only were most people sharing basic facilities in overcrowded tenements or back-to-back houses, so that neighbours inevitably gained quite detailed knowledge about a family's domestic routines and conduct, but the existence of what Williams terms 'a flourishing street acquaintanceship' (1983, p.401) within these localities meant that gossip flowed readily. Indeed, the characteristically close-knit networks developed by those still resident in these areas meant that, once known, information potentially harmful to one's reputation quickly became very public.

Under these circumstances, every effort was needed to ensure that some privacy was maintained. Limiting the home to family and restricting the scope of friendship represents one strategy for doing this. Unlike non-family members, 'family' could generally be relied upon not to spread damaging information. It is not here just a question of their shared past – important though this is. Relatives also have an interest in ensuring that the family name does not get sullied, as the strong ideology of kinship held in these localities might have resulted in their being 'tarred with the same brush'.

The dominant form of sociability occurring in these localities was also shaped by the nature of the gender divisions that occurred within them. These were strongly marked, with males and females routinely leading quite different lives. Within the family, men's responsibilities were mainly seen as those of earning an income. Their work, often arduous and poorly paid, was the main activity around which their lives were built. As the classic studies all emphasise, they were little involved in the details of domestic organisation. For them the home was a place for recuperation, eating and sleeping.

For their wives, on the other hand, the relationship was reversed. Although some were employed on a casual or part-time basis, this was never seen as a major element of their role, even though the income they earned was often crucial for the domestic economy. Instead their overriding responsibility was that of managing the household, often on an inadequate and uncertain income, and servicing the needs of other household members. To a far greater extent, their world was dominated by their home and its environs.

This rigid division of labour tended to be mirrored in the construction of marriage within these localities. While some reports emphasise antagonism and conflict within marriage more than others (e.g., Dennis, Henriques and Slaughter, 1956), all report a majority pattern of marriage being more 'segregated' than 'joint' (Bott, 1957). Within families, each spouse tended to have his or her own tasks and responsibilities with comparatively little overlap or sharing. While during courtship, romantic notions of togetherness may have figured more largely, in practice, most marriages were not of a 'companionate' form, especially after the birth of children. Thus, couples tended not to define their marriages as relationships which would furnish emotional support and personal growth. Marriage was viewed more as a practical arrangement for coordinating domestic and economic activities within which each spouse performed his or her separate yet complementary tasks – and, of course, received differential benefits and rewards.

The division of labour and responsibility within marriage also had an impact on patterns of leisure. With the partial exception of kin gatherings, leisure also tended to be differentiated, with spouses generally not much involved with each other in leisure activities. In the main, husbands tended not to view the home/family complex as a leisure arena, but instead spent much of their free time with other males in non-domestic settings. Female leisure – to the extent that it existed – was oriented much more towards the home, often consisting mainly of sociability with close female kin. Not surprisingly, such a pattern of separate leisure involvement had implications for the nature of the friendships and other non-kin sociable ties that the spouses maintained.

Two consequences are of particular interest. First the sociable relationships – whether termed 'friendships' or otherwise – that each spouse had were likely to be specific to that spouse. Few non-kin relationships were really joint or shared, even though the individuals involved were likely to have been known by both spouses. Secondly, the division of labour and leisure played its part in sustaining the tradition whereby the home was reserved for the family, rather than being used as a site for entertaining others and developing shared friendships. Richard Sennett (1980) expresses this well in discussing the portrayal of friendship in popular literature during the last century. Within this literature, friends, rather than being incorporated into the family circle and becoming friends of the whole family, were largely dissociated from family matters. Indeed, as Sennett writes, friendships provided a means by which males especially could escape from the pressures and demands of the family. Thus, friends were specifically people to go out with, rather than welcome into the home (1980, p.114). So, too, friendships served similar purposes in the traditional working-class communities under discussion here. Rather than celebrating the unity of the couple, their form both mirrored and reinforced the divisions there usually were within marriage.

CONTEMPORARY MIDDLE-CLASS FRIENDSHIP PATTERNS

In such ways, the friendship patterns occurring in traditional working-class communities can be seen to be influenced by the social and economic conditions found within them. Similarly, the characteristic social and economic conditions of middle-class life also shape the form that middle-class sociability and friendship takes. A major element in this, of course, is the greater earning capacity and financial security of middle-class occupations.

Obviously, the readier availability of resources has an effect on the type of life style, including leisure participation, which those involved lead. Equally, though, the advantaged economic position of middle-class people is reflected in their position in the housing market. As well as their homes having better amenities and generally being more comfortable, members of the middle-class have greater choice over the design and location of their housing. Because of the ready availability of mortgage finance to those with secure careers, owner-occupation provides members of this class with a freedom and control over their housing circumstances which people in rented tenures lack.

In addition to being more affluent, the middle class tends to be more geographically mobile than the working class. This greater mobility has two distinct roots. First middle-class careers often entail some degree of geographical mobility. For those characterised by Watson (1964) as 'spiralists', promotion quite frequently involves movement from one plant or office within a company to another located elsewhere, or else a change of company. Even those middle-class people who are in occupations which tie them more to a particular locality – for example, many self-employed professionals – will often have been mobile in the early part of their careers during or immediately after their training.

Apart from their employment patterns, the housing position of the middle class often fosters a degree of geographical mobility. In essence, owner-occupation not only allows freedom of movement, but, especially in times of inflation, encourages mobility as a means of increasing housing quality and wealth-holding. Even though such moves are often within the same general area, they nonetheless tend to limit middle-class people's dependence on particular localities or neighbourhoods. Especially given their readier access to private transport, their circles of sociability are usually quite widely spread. In this respect, the language of 'network' captures the reality of their social involvement far better than that of 'community'.

As a consequence of such factors, members of the middle-class have far fewer difficulties in protecting their personal and familial privacy than do people living in the sort of traditional working-class community discussed in the previous section. Not only are their social worlds less 'local', but most of those who do live near them are likely to know little or nothing about them. Within the neighbourhood, at least, instead of being surrounded by familiars, middle-class residents are surrounded by strangers. To a far greater degree, personal information can be controlled and only revealed to those who are selected. Such information is relatively safe, as networks of gossip do not develop in the locality to the same extent as in more closed, less mobile communities. The material conditions of life are such that, while the developing of an element of cooperation and friendliness with some immediate neighbours may be useful, there is little pressure to generate extensive or overlapping interdependence between those who happen to live in the same neighbourhood. Thus, protecting the privacy of the home and family is relatively easy for the majority most of the time.

So, rather than being embedded in an existing set of interlocking relationships, at a structural level the pattern of middle-class participation is usually more fragmented. One is involved with people in different spheres of activity, but those encountered in each of these spheres have little independent knowledge of other aspects of one's life. The problem for the middle class, then, is not so much protecting privacy and restricting the information to which others have access, but more that of developing significant, personal relationships from those ties which arise within the discrete organisational contexts in which they are involved. To put this another way, the structural conditions of middle-class social existence lead to an emphasis on the deliberate *making* of friends: on the transformation of contextually specific relationships into ones whose parameters are less narrow, through purposeful involvement in aspects of life otherwise kept separate. Hence, middle-class sociability typically depends on establishing sociable contacts, say, through work or participation in leisure organisations, and then developing some of these in a fashion that clearly celebrates personal commitment above circumstances.

Yet it is not just the 'broadening out' of informal relationships into acknowledged friendships that gives middle-class sociability its distinctive character. Also of consequence is the way in which these relationships are brought into the domestic ambit. The tendency is for middle-class friends to be introduced into the family circle, rather than occupying a separate realm. Clearly, bringing friends into the home is an effective way of 'decontextualising' and extending the parameters of relationships. However, it is a form of sociability which is liable to develop only if other aspects of the domestic/familial complex are congruent with it. In this respect, two aspects of middle-class life styles are particularly relevant: the character of the home and the construction of marriage.

As already noted, their financial security and consequent access to mortgage finance has given members of the middle-class a high degree of control of their housing. In addition, during most life phases, middle-class people have the resources to ensure that their homes are well appointed and well furnished. In general, they possess the facilities and amenities to make them congenial and comfortable, if not luxurious. Yet, while the physical characteristics of the home are important, it is not this alone that patterns the form which sociability takes. What also counts here is the meaning which the home has come to have for the middle class. Rather than simply being an abode, a place in which to sleep and eat, the middle-class home is a living space created by its inhabitants to express, in some measure, their individuality and personal style. Thus, the ordering and arrangement of the home – the use of space within it, its décor, its appearance and layout, etc. – occupy a significant place within middle-class culture.

In marked contrast to traditional working-class communities, the middle-class home serves as a medium for the expression of style and taste, and thus to some degree symbolises the values and aspirations of those who have created it. As with all cultural forms, the choices they make here will be influenced by the fads and fashions of the day – subtly fostered by the various commercial enterprises concerned with home furbishment – but, nonetheless, for many of the middle-class the transformation of a house into a home with an appropriate ambience represents a personal and social statement of some significance. Consequently, in addition to being a private arena from which the world can be shut out, for the middle-class the home also serves as a place of display, not so much in the sense of conspicuous consumption, but more as an expression of identity.

The way in which marriages are usually constructed by the middle-class is also congruent with the use of the home for developing and servicing friendships. Although many studies have now cast doubt on the claim that middle-class marriages are genuinely symmetrical or equal (for telling accounts, see, *inter alia*, Oakley, 1974, and Edgell, 1980), there is certainly a strong acceptance within these marriages of an ideology or ethic of equality and companionship. As Edgell (1980), in particular, clearly demonstrates, such an ideology frequently serves to mystify and disguise the structural basis of power within the relationship. However, it also represents a very different view of marriage from that normally found, for example, in the traditional working-class communities discussed above. Whatever the actual degree of inequality, it is a view which emphasises that the primary basis of marriage lies in the quality of the couple's personal relationship. In other words, marriage entails not just a degree of economic or domestic cooperation, but is a union in which companionship and compatibility are rightly central. According to this ideology, what holds couples together is their desire to be with one another and the mutual support and sustenance they can provide.

As a consequence of such a definition of marriage, most middle-class couples expect to share at least some of their non-domestic leisure time activities. The extent to which this happens will, of course, vary a good deal, depending on a range of factors, including their family phase. In a similar way, there is a normative expectation that the couple will be involved as a couple in sociable relationships. They may not know everyone whom the other spends time with, but they are likely to know and engage sociably with those who are more significant. There is a tendency for couple friendships to form – for individual friends to become, in Sennett's (1980) term, friends of the family. Even in those relationships where this does not happen very fully, it is still likely that, at least on some occasions, the couples will interact as couples. Thus, the couple's individual friendship networks normally overlap to a significant degree, so that in a sense the boundaries between the domestic/familial sphere and the sphere of sociability are far less strong than in the working-class localities discussed previously. In this fashion, the emphasis on companionship in middle-class marriage is quite compatible with the use of the home as a setting for sociability with friends.

Middle-class sociability, of course, occurs in various contexts, not just the home. Undoubtedly, however, the use of the home for entertaining friends, rather than just meeting them on, as it were, 'neutral' ground, is an important feature of it. To round off this section, consider briefly the dinner party, very much a middle-class form of entertaining (Willmott, 1987), and one which illustrates many of the issues referred to above. Clearly, in terms of, say, style, formality and size, the character of dinner parties can vary a good deal. Nonetheless, certain more or less common principles tend to underly their staging. It is these which warrant comment here, as they reflect important aspects of middle-class sociability more generally.

As a form of sociability the dinner party obviously requires a certain level of resource, at least in terms of the food and drink which is to be consumed over the evening's course. Certainly, the meal, which acts as a focus for the evening, normally involves a good deal of effort and expense. The aim is not just to provide sustenance, but to produce a meal which is in some sense out of the ordinary. It involves an element of display of culinary skills, which some can experience as quite daunting. As well as the display involved in the meal, the home itself – or at least some part of it – is also on display. The presentation here is not usually the home as it is lived in, but a tidied, spruced up home, on which a level of order has been imposed. Thus, while being invited into the private sphere, the guests are nonetheless seeing a 'public' version of this private sphere, even though some or all of them may often have seen it in a more jumbled state.

The intention of all this effort is not just to demonstrate the social competence and skills of the host, but rather to generate an ambience in which friendship can be promoted and endorsed. Often the guests themselves are quite close friends of the hosts, but this is not always so. In addition to providing an opportunity for existing friends to get together, the dinner party can act as a forum for developing and augmenting relationships. Thus, for example, new colleagues may be invited round for a meal with their partners, so as to extend the basis of the relationship. Or different sets of friends may be invited together, so that they can have an opportunity to meet one another. In general, while the meal serves as a focus, the chief purpose of the occasion is to provide a relatively open-ended setting in which sociable relationships can be affirmed and expressed. In this respect the dinner party, with its scope for wide-ranging discussion, argument and story-telling, is entirely consonant with the broad-based way in which middle-class friendships are typically defined.

It is also pertinent here to note that, in the main, dinner parties tend to be couple-oriented. This does not so much mean that the unattached are excluded – though sometimes this can indeed be the case. Rather, what is meant is that where people are married, living together or otherwise recognised as a couple, they will almost always hold or go to dinner parties together. These are social occasions which normally assume joint, rather than segregated, leisure activities and patterns of sociability. While this of itself reflects a conjugal ideology which is dominant amongst the middle-class, it also tends to result in those present gaining a broader perspective on each other's interests, foibles and commitments. As argued at length above, allowing the basis of relationships to be extended in such a way is a characteristic aspect of middle-class friendship.

Needless to say, the social organisation of dinner parties could be analysed far more fully. However, sufficient has been said to illustrate the point that whereas dinner parties fit in well with the life style of the middle class, they would be quite foreign to the traditions of at least some sections of the working class. The argument holds more generally: the forms of sociability that arise within populations do not develop haphazardly; they develop in a fashion which is congruent with the material conditions and social organisation of those involved, and thus need to be interpreted against this background.

THE 'NEW' WORKING CLASS

So far, the discussion has been concerned with forms of sociability within traditional working-class localities and amongst the more established middle class. Through contrasting the forms of sociability which routinely occur within these groups, the impact that the wider social structure has upon them can be recognised. This is not to imply an inevitable uniformity in the forms of sociability found amongst people similarly located in the social structure. Obviously, there will be much variation in the detailed patterns which people evolve. The point has only been to argue that some consideration needs to be given to the wider context of social life if distinctions in the form which sociability takes are to be properly understood. Ideally, what are required here are detailed accounts of the way in which variations in different aspects of structural position influence the form that sociability takes. Unfortunately, such accounts do not exist. The middle-class especially have rarely been studied, so that comparatively little is known about the way in which variations in the social and material circumstances of different sections of the middle class affect their sociability. More studies have focused on working-class life, though, again, the demise of community studies over the last twenty or so years has resulted in much of the literature being quite dated.

In this respect, of course, the use of traditional working-class communities, except to draw sharp contrasts, is itself beset with problems. These communities certainly no longer represent a dominant working-class life style, as radical changes in housing and employment have demolished their basis. These communities have been superseded as a result of two major shifts in housing provision. First, post-war housing initiatives led to the development of quite large-scale council estates, usually, though not always, on the peripheries of existing urban areas. Various studies of these estates were undertaken – especially in the late 1950s and early 1960s when they were first developed – many of which involved overt comparisons with the pre-existing traditional communities (Mogey, 1956; Young and Willmott, 1957; Klein, 1965). Secondly, there has been a steady drift over much of the same period from privately rented accommodation into owner-occupation. A proportion of the younger generation of working-class families bought their own homes as mortgages ceased being an exclusively middle-class provision. These households have rarely been researched. However, Williams's (1981, 1983) study of the migration history and strategies of a sample of London households contains some suggestive material on this. His insightful analysis of sociable forms has influenced much of this chapter. What follows draws heavily on his ideas.

Consider first the forms of sociability which have developed on council housing estates. Such estates are, of course, not uniform. Some have been maintained to a high standard, while, through design faults or lack of maintenance, others have deteriorated and become less reputable (Damar, 1974). Similarly, their populations differ depending on local economic circumstances and the allocation policies of the controlling authority. For the sake of contrast with the traditional working-class communities discussed above, the focus here will be on those estates which have been well maintained and principally on households which are not experiencing poverty.

The social conditions and material standards on the new estates were very different from those of the older areas from which most of the initial residents were rehoused. To begin with, those living there were strangers to one another, rather than being familiars. Most of their kin and acquaintances had either stayed in the old localities or else been rehoused in other estates. Consequently, few of the residents knew anything about their new neighbours. Nor did they have the same need to cooperate with them at a daily level, as each household had its own domestic amenities, rather than having to share them communally. Over time, greater knowledge of each other's circumstances developed, but rarely to the extent common in the traditional communities. Similarly, as children became adult, even those who remained in the area were not necessarily housed close by, so that extensive local kinship networks rarely developed as they had done in the older localities. In some ways, this mattered less for the more affluent households, as the growth of car ownership made distance less of a constraint.

At the same time, the different domestic architecture of the new houses, the amenities and facilities they contained, and the increasing affluence generated both by better paid jobs and the prevalence of wives' employment meant that the home itself became more congenial as a social arena. In conjunction with the relative absence of public and communal leisure facilities – not least pubs – on the estates, and the growth of home entertainments, the thrust was for the family as a whole to spend more time together within the home. While the changes can be easily romanticised, the movement from, as it were, a 'street-centred' existence to a 'home-centred' one was also fostered by contingent changes in the character of familial relationships. In particular, while husbands continued to have far more freedom than their wives, the ideology of marriage being a relationship premised on companionship and sharing became accepted more generally. So, too, there was an increased emphasis on the active interest that fathers should take in their children's personal development (Harris, 1977; Allan, 1985; Holme, 1985).

These shifts have some implications for the form that sociability typically takes. To begin with, the kin group is likely to be more dispersed, so that interaction will be less routine and less frequent. Of course, particular ties retain their significance, but their interactional format is likely to be different from that reported for the traditional communities. In some cases, for example, the couple's closest companions may be a sibling and their spouse, with a range of sociable activities being arranged between them (Allan, 1977b). The availability of a car can, of course, be crucial in facilitating this where the siblings do not live close together.

The form that non-kin sociability takes is also likely to be influenced by the new conditions of these estates. Interestingly, in Willmott's (1963) study of Dagenham – one of the few studies to focus on the patterns which emerge after a long period of settlement – there was evidence that the 'boundaries' constructed around the home were a little more permeable than in the traditional working-class communities. While the friendships that people had still tended to be relatively restricted in context in comparison with middle-class patterns, the home was on occasion used for entertaining non-kin. While there is a need for rather more information than is currently available, it would seem likely that, at least in more affluent working-class households, this tendency will become more marked. With increased expenditure on home furbishment and entertainment, and a greater expectation of companionship and shared leisure within marriage, it is likely that this section of the working class will come more to define the home as an appropriate arena for socialising with friends (Holme, 1985; Willmott, 1987).

The second section of the working class to be considered here consists of those who have become owner-occupiers, rather than council tenants. As noted earlier, the readier availability of mortgages (and more recently the discounted sales of council houses) has meant that some sections of the working class have been able to purchase their own homes. This, in turn, has allowed them greater flexibility and choice over the location of their housing than is usually available to either private or council tenants. However, as also noted, few studies have examined the impact of owner-occupation on the social lives of these working-class households. A partial exception here is Williams's (1983) study of households in London. His concern was principally with the impact of migration on kin and non-kin relationships. However, while his data is neither limited to the working-class nor to owner-occupiers, it is suggestive of some of the changes in sociable patterns that are likely to emerge as sections of the working class purchase houses, especially on the residential outskirts of urban areas.

Williams's (1981) study demonstrates that, at least within London, households which are geographically mobile do not, as a consequence, necessarily lose contact with their kin. Indeed, on the contrary, sections of primary kin networks may deliberately maintain their cohesion through their all migrating outwards in more or less the same direction, either in what he terms a pattern of chain migration or as part of a 'stepwise movement' (Williams, 1983, p.389).

In the former case, the kin group move to a new locality in the footsteps of a 'pathfinder' who has already moved to the area and become established. Stepwise movement, on the other hand, involves one member of a kin group migrating to a new area, in most cases not that far from their initial starting point, to be followed some time later by a sibling or parent who moves further out along approximately the same geographic sector. At a later stage still, another kin member, or indeed the initial migrant household, may similarly move further out on the same rough axis. In Williams's sample such stepwise movement was quite common, allowing migration to occur over relatively long distances without groups of kin becoming too dispersed to provide each other with active support. The 'stepwise' housing strategy is, of course, not equally available to everyone. In the main, it is the more, rather than less, affluent who will have the possibility of organising their housing in this way. In Williams's study, this pattern of migration was not solely restricted to owner-occupiers, but amongst the working class it was a pattern which mainly involved the households of more skilled manual workers. Indeed, a minority of these outward moving working-class families had middle-class connections or aspirations (Williams, 1983, p.402). Almost certainly, from what is known from other studies, as well as from Williams's examples, they would all tend to be households which placed a good deal of emphasis on status and valued their respectability highly. It is equally likely that most of the married couples involved perceived their marriage in companionate terms and defined their homes as quite central to their lives.

As Williams emphasises, the forms of friendship developed by these outward moving working-class respondents were quite different from those reported by his other working-class respondents. Whereas these latter tended to restrict the scope of their non-kin sociability to specific contexts, mirroring the traditional working-class pattern found elsewhere, the outwardly mobile respondents had a more diffuse, 'middle-class' conception of friendship. At least some of their friendships were not defined in terms of, or constrained by, a single context, but instead were activated more widely. Important within this, these people did not define the home solely as a preserve of the family or the kin group. Instead, friends were invited back to the home and were entertained in it. In this respect, there was more of an overlap between kin and friends than is the case with other sections of the working class (Williams, 1983).

Williams suggests two main reasons why a 'stepwise' pattern of outward migration should lead to the development of more diffuse forms of friendship than appear usual with other sections of the working class. First, because each individual move that people made was over a relatively short range – normally their new homes were broadly within the area covered by their existing leisure travel (Williams, 1981) – they were able to maintain contact quite readily with their previous acquaintances. However, because of the element of geographical separation now involved, the visits they made to these acquaintances tended to be to their homes and consequently led to a reformulation of the ties into friendships *per se*. Secondly, successive episodes of geographical mobility led to the sociable networks of those involved being quite dispersed. As a consequence, the set of friends did not have the opportunity to form tightly knit groups or cliques which could exercise strong informal control over their members. Thus, the relationships that were sustained were more 'individualised', following the mould of friendship rather than mateship.

Williams is quite right to argue that the very different social conditions of his outward moving working-class families influence their patterns of sociability. The fact that they are not involved in neighbourhood communities certainly makes it likely that their informal ties will be patterned differently from those of his working-class respondents still living in London's Victorian boroughs. Yet the extent to which any particular episode of short range or 'stepwise' geographical mobility *of itself* is responsible for the development of a friendship form of sociable tie can be questioned. In principle, at least, journeys made back to previous residential localities need not involve home visiting. Especially if fairly frequent visits are made in order to see kin still living in the area, then any non-kin contacts previously restricted to a specific context could presumably continue to be serviced in a modified form within those contexts. As an example, mates previously seen regularly in a pub could still be met at that pub during whatever visits are made to parents or siblings living nearby.

The point here is that the pattern of 'stepwise' mobility is likely to be part of a wider mosaic. As suggested earlier, the use of the home for entertaining friends on a regular basis almost certainly involves a more companionate than segregated ideology of marriage. Indeed, it could be that such an ideology, with its emphasis on the unity of the spouses, is highly characteristic of couples who decide to engage in repeated mobility. Also, as noted above, allowing friends into the home on a casual basis entails a conception of the domestic sphere in which the boundaries between private and public are relatively 'open', a matter which is itself likely to be related to the material standards that prevail. In essence, the argument here is that while mobility plays some part in shaping the form that sociability takes, other, albeit related, factors are also of consequence in generating particular outcomes.

CONCLUSION

The data on which this chapter has drawn have, to put it mildly, been uneven. The available material on the form that sociability takes in traditional working-class communities of the type found in the late 1950s is quite full and sufficiently cohesive to allow generalisations to be made with some confidence. However, as noted above, these communities no longer exist in the form they once did, as the occupational and housing conditions that generated them have been superseded over the last two generations. In the 1980s there is renewed concern over the problems of the inner city, but the social conditions of these areas are not equivalent to those reported in the older urban community studies. Though less comprehensive, information is also available about the forms of sociability that typically occur on the purpose-built council estates which have been constructed since the war. On the other hand, there are relatively few studies of sociability amongst more affluent sections of the working class, especially those in owner-occupation, or amongst different sections of the middle class. Similarly, at the other end of the housing scale, there is little information about the way in which homelessness affects patterns of friendship, despite the increasing number of families in bed and breakfast accommodation.

As a consequence, the analysis of sociable forms presented in this chapter has necessarily been quite superficial. A good deal more empirical material would be necessary if the ideas it proposes were to be developed at all fully. Nonetheless, the basic thrust of the argument should be evident. The form that sociability typically takes – that is, the way in which informal relationships are routinely organised and patterned and the boundaries that are constructed around these relationships, defining what is included and excluded – is not simply a matter of individual decision. Rather, the form which an individual's sociable relationships take is influenced by that person's social and material situation. Although related to the discussion in Chapter 3, it needs to be emphasised that the prime argument here does not concern the way an individual's opportunities for developing and sustaining sociable ties are structured. Instead it is an argument about the manner in which those sociable relationships which do occur are patterned.

To quite a large degree, the central matter here concerns the boundaries or parameters that are placed around sociable relationships by those involved. The issue is the way in which these ties are typically 'framed': the implicit rules governing what is taken as relevant to them and what lies outside their orbit. One important element in this is the extent to which the tie involves knowledge of and access to the private sphere of the home, or is contained more in public settings. While inviting people into the home does not necessarily involve a greater willingness to divulge highly personal or sensitive information, it is indicative of a more broadly based and inclusive relationship.

Obviously, home visiting of itself is only one factor in this. The actual style of entertaining, the formality or informality of the interaction, the rooms to which people are allowed access, the extent to which the home is deliberately transformed for the occasion, and so on, are also of significance. All that is being claimed here is that different manners of socialising tend to develop amongst people and groups depending on their different social and material situation. Factors like housing conditions, economic standing, marital relationship, neighbourhood involvement, social and geographical mobility all play a part in shaping the parameters typically placed around sociability.

Of course, far more research is required if the relationship between forms of sociability and these wider issues is to be understood properly. As yet, there is rather limited information about the different forms that friendship can take. Much of the information we have is now quite old, and is in any case quite partial, covering some groups in the population, but not others. Certainly, it would be helpful to have more information about the way the framing of friendship alters – if it does – over the life course, or about the differences there are between ethnic groups, as well as more about those class sections which have been less fully researched.

The gap, though, is not just in the groups that researchers have covered. There is also the problem of the questions researchers pose and, in a sense, the seriousness with which they examine sociability. The tendency, especially in large-scale survey research, is still for the notion of friendship to be treated in a simplistic fashion: a friend is a friend is a friend. Although the data is far from full, it is evident that researchers need to be sensitive to the variations that exist in the way in which sociability is typically organised. They then need to build these distinctions into their accounts, if our understanding of the role of friendship in social life is to develop. Likewise, a case can be made that researchers studying other aspects of social organisation should concern themselves more with patterns of sociability and friendship than they currently do. Despite all the theoretical and methodological criticisms they rightly attracted, the 'traditional' community studies of the 1950s and 1960s provide something of a model for the sociology of friendship here.

Whatever else their faults, their integrative, holistic framework did at least allow the material and social context of friendship to be appreciated in a way that relatively few contemporary studies do.

9

CONCLUSION

Over the last ten years or so, there has been renewed interest amongst social researchers – and, in particular social psychologists – in the study of different forms of personal relationships. Following the lead given by such investigators as Michael Argyle, Steve Duck and Daniel Perlman, the field of personal relationships has become something of a growth area, with new academic journals appearing and regular international conferences being organised. Indeed, there are arguments that a new 'science of relationships', bridging the traditional divisions between academic disciplines, is developing (Duck and Perlman, 1985).

Such a claim appears reasonably well-founded from the viewpoint of psychology. Certainly, there has been quite a radical shift in recent years from a predominant concern with rather narrow issues such as, say, attitude similarities among friendship dyads, or liking and personal attraction amongst strangers. Psychologists and cognate researchers are now adopting a much broader perspective on the varied development of a range of different personal relationships across the life course. Moreover, their empirical data on relationships relies far less heavily on laboratory manipulation than it has in the past. Instead, those studying personal relationships have spread their net more widely and examined existing relationships in their natural contexts. At least in the area of personal relationship, the jibe that psychology is mainly concerned with the behaviour of undergraduate students in the laboratory is no longer entirely legitimate.

Yet, from a sociological standpoint, arguments that a new interdisciplinary science of relationships is developing, which supersedes previous research orientations, are less convincing. In large part this is because the substantive and methodological innovations being claimed are not so novel within the discipline of sociology. The shift by psychologists from a focus on pseudo-relations in laboratory settings to the study of real ties within their social context is certainly welcome, but it does not in any sense represent a new direction for sociological approaches to personal relationships. Sociologists have customarily studied quite a wide range of personal relationships and, by the nature of their discipline, have attempted to locate them within their relevant social context.

Moreover, in the main, the new approach to personal relationships advanced by psychologists remains, not surprisingly, embedded in the domain of their discipline. In other words, the dominant concerns still tend to be oriented towards the individual, rather than towards aspects of social structure. For instance, the focus is on feeling states, motivation, relational skills, and so on, albeit studied as process in a far more sophisticated fashion than previously. To put this somewhat differently, the thrust tends to be on relationships as *personal* rather than *social* constructions. In consequence, the questions posed are often ones which are not particularly germane to a sociological analysis of personal ties.

In contrast, this book has been specifically concerned with the social character of friendship in its various guises. Rather than focusing on the emotional significance of friendship or, say, attraction processes within friendship, the aim has been to portray the sociological dimension of friendship and to argue that friendship is not only a personal matter, but one which is inherently social as well. In essence, there have been two aspects to this argument developed in the previous chapters. The first of these is that friendship is not just a voluntary or freely chosen relationship. It is one which is patterned and structured in a variety of ways by factors which can be recognised, at least to some degree, as genuinely social and lying outside the individual's immediate control. The second strand of the argument focuses on the social utility of friendship ties. The aim here has been to suggest that, in addition to bestowing emotional and other such benefits, ties of friendship are also significant in relation to the wider organisation of social life.

Because friendship is commonly defined as being voluntary and freely chosen, the extent to which it is shaped by social factors is often underplayed, both in everyday life and in the academic literature. Yet ties of friendship are socially patterned at a variety of levels. As developed in Chapter 3, one factor affecting people's involvement in ties of friendship is the 'space' there is in their lives for sociability. In part, this refers to the way in which other aspects of people's lives – the character of their work commitments and domestic obligations, their material circumstances and existing relationships – encourage or limit the opportunities they have to meet others who are socially defined as suitable for friendship. More importantly, though, the 'space' individuals have in their lives for friendship will also pattern the way in which the various friendship ties they have generated are serviced.

The friendships an individual is involved in are not, therefore, independent of other facets of his or her life. On the contrary, they need to be understood against the background of opportunities and constraints for sociability built into that person's daily routines. A range of different factors will bear on this, with no single element normally dominating. What matters, as argued at some length in Chapter 3, is the immediate social environment – the overall constellation of factors shaping the freedom and, to some extent, desires he or she has to engage in sociability. It is this which needs to be examined if the nature of people's involvement in friendships is to be understood adequately.

However, it is not just the opportunities that an individual has for developing or servicing friendships which are socially structured. A person's immediate social environment is also likely to influence the 'content' of his or her sociable ties and, indeed, the form they take. At the most obvious level, the matters friends discuss with one another and the common interests they have will be affected by their position in the social structure. Issues which are quite central to one person's life may be of little concern to another and lie outside his or her experience. In some measure the content of friendships may be a matter of personal preference and choice, but, at the very least, the interests people have – i.e. their preferences and choices – will bear some relationship to their structural location and the way in which this patterns their common routines and experiences. Hunt and Satterlee's (1987) discussion of the different topics of conversation occurring amongst customers in the pubs they studied provides a good illustration of this.

The organisation of sociable ties – the form they take – is also likely to be influenced by the social position of those involved. This issue of how boundaries are drawn around friendships, of what is included or excluded from them, has been discussed at some length in the book. Although there are major gaps in the analysis, the discussion in Chapter 8 was an attempt to indicate how the dominant forms which sociable relationships take are shaped by the material and social circumstances that prevail in people's lives. People's perception of their home, the character of their marriage, their economic standing, their residential histories, their work commitments and obligations, and the like, all interact to influence the manner in which sociable ties are enacted and the boundaries constructed around them.

So, too, the literature reviewed in Chapter 5 indicated that men and women quite regularly appear to have somewhat different orientations to friendship. Although these differences can be over-emphasised (Wright, 1982), in general, women seem more willing than men to talk through personal issues with their friends. Men's sociability, in contrast, tends to be framed more around common activities. In part, this may be a result of their different socialisation in childhood, but, as argued in Chapter 5, it is also a consequence of the different social positions the genders typically occupy, and the continued support given in adulthood to dominant notions of masculinity and femininity. In this, the 'content' of women's friendships reflects the issues which tend to dominate their lives. Their greater willingness to confide in their friends, disclose their feelings and discuss domestic or personal problems can be recognised as broadly congruent with what is often their predominant social identity as 'home-maker' routinely responsible for the 'expressive' management of family life.

The second major theme of the book has been that friendships are incorporated into the organisation of social life far more than is usually acknowledged in the research literature. The marked tendency to view friendship as essentially a personal relationship leads to an emphasis on the psychological and emotional benefits it bestows on the individual. Its role within the social realm is consequently often underplayed. This point was developed most fully in Chapter 4. There it was argued that friends, generically defined, often act as a resource that can be drawn on to help people achieve their particular goals or cope with the contingencies they face. That is to say, friendship often has a social utility which is quite central to its character. This aspect of friendship is often pushed into the background, no doubt partly because at a cultural level the relationship is not supposed to be defined in instrumental terms.

At a social level, friendship's part in integrating people socially is obviously important. The companionship of friends provides individuals with a sense of belonging and, as it were, a link with the wider society. Less abstractly, friends, in whatever form they take, are often drawn on to help meet the different demands that individuals routinely or otherwise face. This may involve discussing issues and providing advice; it may mean helping out with some specific task; it may require using particular skills or contacts. Whatever the actual content – and, of course, this will depend in part on the social position of those involved – the point is that friends assist each other in a variety of ways in order to further their interests or handle the contingencies they face. Finally, in Chapter 4, it was argued that friends play some part in moulding an individual's self-identity. As Jerrome (1984) shows so well, friends can provide a sense of freedom from formal role positions without undermining or threatening these in any major way. Because they are set apart from institutionalised arrangements, friends can reaffirm the significance of an individual's social standing, while still fostering a sense of personal distinctiveness and worth.

Yet, whereas friends are routinely used in a variety of ways, there are certainly situations where asking friends for assistance can pose problems. To begin with, some forms of help may be seen as lying outside the boundaries that implicitly define the relationship, so that asking for aid in these circumstances is inappropriate. Moreover, as emphasised throughout the book, friendship – however defined – is essentially a relationship of equality. Consequently, there is frequently a resistance against making too many claims on a friend unless they can be repaid in some way. A number of the processes involved in this were discussed in Chapter 7. That chapter, and to a lesser extent Chapter 6, also illustrated some of the tensions that arise in friendships when one side's social position alters significantly. When this occurs to a degree sufficient to affect the broad status similarity typically found in friendship, there tends to be a gradual withdrawal from the tie. Consequently, as was evident in the different examples discussed in Chapter 7, in the longer run 'routine' or 'run-of-the-mill' friendships tend to dissipate in times of major change and be less supportive than idealised images of friendship imply.

STUDYING FRIENDSHIP

A major aim of this book has been to demonstrate that friendship and other such informal relations are interesting from a sociological viewpoint and worth studying. As argued above, they are not just of personal consequence, but also important within the routines of social organisation. Yet, overall, the topic of friendship has received relatively little attention from sociologists. Certainly, far more research would be required if the set of questions that were raised in Chapter 1 is to receive adequate answers. Similarly, from the discussion in Chapter 8, it is evident that we know rather little about the friendship patterns of quite significant sections of the population. Moreover, much of the existing material on sociability is now rather old.

Thus, there is a need for more empirical material on the organisation and management of friendship, on its social patterning and the use to which these ties are put. In the past, useful – though hardly complete – information on these matters was provided in community and occupational studies. In part, the unfashionability of the 'traditional' kind of community study has meant that information on patterns of sociability is no longer reported in the way it once was. While many studies of different aspects of social life certainly still touch on friendship, relatively few make it an explicit topic of interest or develop an analysis of its impact or organisation.

This, of course, raises the question of what sort of research is most appropriate for further developing a sociology of friendship. At one level, there is a need simply for more information about the extent to which people are involved with others in friendships and similar social ties. Such information can be provided by large-scale representative surveys inquiring into the nature and extent of friendship ties. However, such surveys often do not actually reveal a great deal about the character or social significance of these relationships, frequently because they concentrate too much on a small number of 'close' or 'best' friendships.

As discussed earlier in the book, this tends to encourage a somewhat idealised portrayal of friendship, both by the respondent and in the analysis. Furthermore, and perhaps most importantly, this form of investigation also makes it difficult to locate the friendships in their social context. Yet, without this being done, it is difficult to appreciate the real significance of friendships in people's lives. Again here, discussing friendship in the abstract probably encourages an idealised, or at least normatively acceptable, presentation of its character. As a consequence, it is likely that issues to do with compatibility or emotional support will be focused on more than, say, questions about the practical use routinely made of friends.

Many of these problems have been overcome in less structured, small-scale research. Usually these studies are also mainly based on interviewing, but because they are more intensive and focus on well-defined sections of the population, they allow a fuller appreciation of the social significance of friendship in people's lives. But, as well as situating ties of friendship within the individual's overall circumstances, a number of small-scale studies have also benefited from being able to examine the dynamics of friendship within particular social contexts.

A number of advantages can accrue from basing research around specifically defined settings. First, such research may enable a range of sociable ties to be examined, not just those approximating most closely to 'true' friendship. Secondly, it may be possible to obtain accounts from both sides of a friendship, rather than having to rely on a unilateral version. Thirdly, opportunities may arise to observe different friendships in action, thereby not just allowing some check on the accounts given in interviews, but also enabling aspects of the friendship which tend to be taken for granted to be studied. Most important, though, conducting small-scale, 'situated' studies of friendship means that contextual issues can be considered in the analysis, thereby allowing the place of friendship within social organisation to be better understood.

The argument here is that the social significance of friendship will be more evident in studies which are grounded to some degree in particular contexts than where questions are posed in a generalised or abstract form. For this reason, much interesting information on the working of friendship can be obtained from studies in which friendship itself is not the main focus. As already mentioned, occupational and community studies have frequently provided quite rich pickings for those seeking to analyse friendship patterns. Without too much change of direction, studies in many other areas could also contribute much to our knowledge of friendship matters. For instance, research into work settings, domestic life, political and religious organisations, leisure activities, cultural conformity or deviance – amongst other issues – can provide an opportunity to explore the influence and nature of friendship ties. By considering informal ties more systematically than they usually do, such studies may well add an important dimension to their substantive analyses, in addition to providing material for friendship research.

As a final comment here, it is worth emphasising the need for more studies that examine the role of friends, and other informal ties, at times of personal change. A number of issues relevant to this were raised in Chapters 6 and 7 in the discussions of widowhood, unemployment and divorce. Yet, clearly, there is scope for far more research concerned with the influence of, and impact on, friendships of the various changes that people experience over their life course. In particular, there is a need for studies over time, so that changes in friend relationships can be properly monitored. However, this is an area of friendship research which has been noticeably weak. There have been some retrospective analyses of friendship, mainly concerned with the elderly, but very few studies which actively trace how and why friendship behaviour and networks are modified as people's circumstances alter. Indeed, generally, notwithstanding the obvious methodological difficulties entailed, more longitudinal studies of friendship would be of great benefit and would undoubtedly add much to our knowledge of the role of friendship in social life.

BIBLIOGRAPHY

Adams, B. N. (1967), 'Interaction theory and the social network', *Sociometry*, 30: pp.50–9.

Adams, R. G. (1985), 'People would talk: normative barriers to cross-sex friendships for elderly women', *The Gerontologist*, 25: pp.605–11.

Adams, R. G. (1986), 'Secondary friendship networks and psychological well-being among elderly women', *Activities, Adaptation and Aging*, 8: pp.59–72.

Adams, R. G. (1987), 'Patterns of network change: a longitudinal study of friendships of elderly women', *The Gerontologist*, 27: pp.222–7.

Allan, G. A. (1977a), 'Class variations in friendship patterns', *British Journal of Sociology*, 28: pp.389–93.

Allan, G. A. (1977b), 'Sibling solidarity', *Journal of Marriage and the Family*, 39: pp.177–84.

Allan, G. A. (1979), *A Sociology of Friendship and Kinship*, Allen & Unwin, London.

Allan, G. A. (1985), *Family Life: Domestic Roles and Social Organisation*, Blackwell, Oxford.

Allan, G. A. (1986), 'Friendship and care for elderly people', *Ageing and Society*, 6: pp.1–12.

Babchuk, N. (1965), 'Primary friends and kin: a study of the associations of middle class couples', *Social Forces*, 43: pp. 483–93.

Bankoff, E. A. (1981), 'Effects of friendship support on the psychological well-being of widows', in H. Z. Lopata and D. Maines (eds), *Research in the Interweave of Social Roles: Friendship*, Jai Press, Greenwich, Conn.

Banton, M. (1966), *The Social Anthropology of Complex Societies*, Tavistock, London.

Barnes, J. A. (1954), 'Class and committees in a Norwegian island parish', *Human Relations*, 7: pp.39–58.

Barnhart, E. (1976), 'Friends and lovers in a lesbian counterculture community', in N. Glazer-Malbin (ed), *Old Family/New Family: Interpersonal Relationships*, Van Nostrand, New York.

Bates, A. (1964), 'Privacy – a useful concept?', *Social Forces*, 42: pp.429–34.

Bates A. and Babchuk, N. (1961), 'The primary group: a re-appraisal', *Sociological Quarterly*, 2: pp.181–91.

Becker, G. (1980), *Growing Old in Silence*, University of California Press, Berkeley.

Bell, C. and Newby, H. (1971), *Community Studies*, Allen & Unwin, London.

Bell, R. (1976), 'Swinging: separating the sexual from friendship', in N. Glazer-Malbin (ed), *Old Family/New Family: Interpersonal Relationships*, Van Nostrand, New York.

Bell, R. (1981), *Worlds of Friendship*, Sage, Beverly Hills.

Berger, P. (1966), *Invitation to Sociology*, Penguin, Harmondsworth.

Binney, V., Harkell, G. and Nixon, J. (1985), 'Refuges and housing for battered women', in J. Pahl (ed), *Private Violence and Public Policy*, Routledge & Kegan Paul, London.

Binns, D. and Mars, G. (1984), 'Family, community and unemployment: a study in change', *Sociological Review*, 32: pp.662–95.

Blau, Z. (1961), 'Structural constraints on friendship in old age', *American Sociological Review*, 26: pp.429–39.

Blau, Z. (1973), *Old Age in a Changing Society*, Franklin Watts, New York.

Boissevain, J. (1974), *Friends of Friends*, Blackwell, Oxford.

Boissevain, J. and Mitchell, J. C. (eds) (1973), *Network Analysis: Studies in Human Interaction*, Mouton, The Hague.

Booth, A. (1972), 'Sex and social participation', *American Sociological Review*, 37: pp.183–92.

Booth, A. and Hess, E. (1974), 'Cross-sex friendship', *Journal of Marriage and the Family*, 36: pp.38–47.

Bott, E. (1957, 1971), *Family and Social Network*, Tavistock, London.

Boulton, M. G. (1983), *On Being a Mother*, Tavistock, London.

Brah, A. (1986), 'Unemployment and racism: Asian youth on the dole', in S. Allen, A. Watson, K. Purcell and S. Wood (eds), *The Experience of Unemployment*, Macmillan, Basingstoke.

Brain, R. (1976), *Friends and Lovers*, Hart-Davis, MacGibbon, London.

Briggs, A. and Oliver, J. (eds) (1985), *Caring: Experiences of Looking After Disabled Relatives*, Routledge & Kegan Paul, London.

Bulmer, M. (1986), *Neighbours: The Work of Philip Abrams*, Cambridge University Press, Cambridge.

Burridge, K. (1957), 'Friendship in Tangu', *Oceania*, 27: pp.177–89.

Caldwell M. A. and Peplau, L. A. (1982), 'Sex differences in same-sex friendships', *Sex Roles*, 8: pp.721–32.

Calnan, M. (1983), 'Social networks and patterns of help-seeking behaviour', *Social Science and Medicine*, 17: pp.25–8.

Cecil. R., Offer, J. and St. Leger, F. (1987), *Informal Welfare: A Sociological Study of Care in Northern Ireland*, Gower, Aldershot.

Chappell, N. (1983), 'Informal support among the elderly', *Research on Aging*, 5: pp.77–99.

Chester, R. (1977), 'The one-parent family: deviant or variant?', in R. Chester and J. Peel (eds), *Equalities and Inequalities in Family Life*, Academic Press, London.

Chibnall, S. and Saunders, P. (1977), 'Worlds apart: notes on the social reality of corruption', *British Journal of Sociology*, 28: pp.138–54.

Clark, M. (1978), 'The unemployed on supplementary benefit', *Journal of Social Policy*, 7: pp.385–410.

Coates, K. and Silburn, R. (1970), *Poverty: The Forgotten Englishmen*, Penguin, Harmondsworth.

Coenen-Huther, J. (1987), 'Encounter between ethnology and sociology: the case of joking relationships', *International Sociology*, 2: pp.27–43.

Coffield, F., Borrill, C. and Marshall, S. (1986), *Growing Up at the Margins*, Open University Press, Milton Keynes.

Cohen, C. I. and Rajkowski, H. (1982), 'What's in a friend? substantive and theoretical issues', *The Gerontologist*, 22: pp.261–6.

Cohen, Y. (1961), 'Patterns of friendship' in Y. Cohen (ed), *Social Structure and Personality*, Holt, Rinehart and Winston, New York.

Cornwell, J. (1984), *Hard-Earned Lives*, Tavistock, London.

Coyle, A. (1984), *Redundant Women*, Women's Press, London.

Cragg, A. and Dawson, T. (1984), *Unemployed Women: A Study of Attitudes and Experiences*, Department of Employment Research Paper No. 37.

Crozier, M. (1964), *The Bureaucratic Phenomenon*, University of Chicago Press, Chicago.

Damar, S. (1974), 'Wine Alley: the sociology of a dreadful enclosure', *Sociological Review*, 22: pp.221–48.

Deem, R. (1982), 'Women, leisure and inequality', *Leisure Studies*, 1: pp.229–46.

Deem, R. (1986), *All Work and No Play*, Open University Press, Milton Keynes.

Delphy, C. (1984), *Close to Home: A Materialist Analysis of Women's Oppression*, Hutchinson, London.

Dennis, N., Henriques, F. and Slaughter, C. (1956), *Coal Is Our Life*, Tavistock, London.

Dickens, W. J. and Perlman, D. (1981), 'Friendship over the life cycle', in S. Duck and R. Gilmour (eds), *Personal Relationships 2: Developing Personal Relationships*, Academic Press, London.

Dixey, R. and Talbot, M. (1982), *Women, Leisure and Bingo*, Trinity and All Saints College, Leeds.

Dobash, R. E. and Dobash, R. (1980), *Violence Against Wives: A Case Against the Patriarchy*, Open Books, London.

Dobash, R. E. and Dobash, R. (1984), 'The nature and antecedents of violent events', *British Journal of Criminology*, 24: pp. 269–88.

Dobash, R. E., Dobash, R. and Cavanagh, K. (1985), 'The contact between battered women and social and medical agencies', in J. Pahl (ed), *Private Violence and Public Policy*, Routledge & Kegan Paul, London.

Douvan, E. and Adelson, J. (1966), *The Adolescent Experience*, Wiley, New York.

Duck, S. and Perlman, D. (eds) (1985), *Understanding Personal Relationships*, Sage, Beverly Hills.

Edgell, S. (1980), *Middle Class Couples*, Allen & Unwin, London.

Edgerton, R. B. (1967), *The Cloak of Competence*, University of California Press, Berkeley.

Elias, N. (1973), 'Towards a theory of communities', in C. Bell and H. Newby (eds), *The Sociology of Community*, Cass, London.

Equal Opportunities Commission (1982), *Caring for the Elderly and Handicapped*, Equal Opportunities Commission, Manchester.

Fallding, H. (1961), 'The family and the idea of a cardinal role', *Human Relations*, 14: pp.329–50.

Finch, J. (1983), *Married to the Job*, Allen & Unwin, London.

Finch, J. and Groves, D. (1980), 'Community care and the family: a case for equal opportunities?', *Journal of Social Policy*, 9: pp.486–511.

Finch, J. and Groves, D. (eds) (1983), *A Labour of Love*, Routledge & Kegan Paul, London.

Fine, G. A. (1986), 'Friendships in the work place', in V. J. Derlega and B. A. Winstead (eds), *Friendship and Social Interaction*, Springer-Verlag, New York.

Finer Report (1974), *Report of the Committee on One-Parent Families*, HMSO, London.

Fischer, C. S. (1982), *To Dwell Among Friends*, University of Chicago Press, Chicago.

Fischer, C. S., Jackson, R. M., Stueve, C. A., Gerson, K. and Jones, L. M. (1977), *Networks and Places: Social Relations in the Urban Setting*, Free Press, New York.

Fischer, C. S. and Oliker, S. J. (1983), 'A research note on friendship, gender and the life cycle', *Social Forces*, 62: pp.124–33.

Fox, M., Gibbs, M. and Auerbach, D. (1985), 'Age and gender dimensions of friendship', *Psychology of Women Quarterly*, 9: pp.489–502.

Gamarnikow, E., Morgan, D., Purvis, J. and Taylorson, D. (1983), *Gender, Class and Work*, Heinemann, London.

Glendinning, C. (1983), *Unshared Care: Parents and Their Disabled Children*, Routledge & Kegan Paul, London.

Goffman, E. (1959), *The Presentation of Self in Everyday Life*. Doubleday Anchor, Garden City, New York.

Granovetter, M. (1973), 'The strength of weak ties', *American Journal of Sociology*, 78: pp.1360–80.

Griffin, C. (1985), *Typical Girls? Young Women from School to the Job Market*, Routledge & Kegan Paul, London.

Harris, C. C. (1969), *The Family*, Allen & Unwin, London.

Harris, C. C. (1977), 'Changing conceptions of the relation between family and societal form in western society', in R. Scase (ed), *Industrial Society: Class, Cleavage and Control*, Allen & Unwin, London.

Harris, C. C. (1987), *Redundancy and Recession in South Wales*, Blackwell, Oxford.

Hart, N. (1976), *When Marriage Ends*, Tavistock, London.

Hess, B. B. (1972), 'Friendship', in M. W. Riley, M. Johnson and A. Foner (eds), *Aging and Society, Vol. 3: A Sociology of Age Stratification*, Russell Sage, New York.

Hess, B. B. (1979), 'Sex roles, friendship and the life course', *Research on Aging*, 1: pp.494–515.

Hobson, D. (1978), 'Housewives: isolation as oppression', in Women's Study Group, Centre for Contemporary Cultural Studies, *Women Take Issue*, Hutchinson, London.

Holme, A. (1985), *Housing and Young Families in East London*, Routledge & Kegan Paul, London.

Homer, M., Leonard, A. and Taylor. P. (1984), *Private Violence: Public Shame*, Cleveland Refuge and Aid for Women and Children, Cleveland.

Homer, M., Leonard, A. and Taylor, P. (1985). 'Personal relationships: help and hindrance', in N. Johnson (ed), *Marital Violence*, Sociological Review Monograph 31, Routledge & Kegan Paul, London.

Hunt, G. and Satterlee, S. (1987), 'Darts, drinks and the pub: the culture of female drinking', *Sociological Review*, 35: pp.575–601.

Hunt, P. (1978), 'Cash transactions and household tasks', *Sociological Review*, 26: pp.555–71.

Hunt, P. (1980), *Gender and Class Consciousness*, Macmillan, Basingstoke.

Jackson, R. M. (1977), 'Social structure and process in friendship choice', in C. S. Fischer, R. M. Jackson, C. A. Stueve, K. Gerson and L. M. Jones (eds), *Networks and Places: Social Relations in the Urban Setting*, Free Press, New York.

Jackson, R. M., Fischer, C. S. and Jones, L. M. (1977), 'The dimensions of social networks', in C. S. Fischer, R. M. Jackson, C. A. Stueve, K. Gerson and L. M. Jones (eds), *Networks and Places: Social Relations in the Urban Setting*, Free Press, New York.

Jenkins, R., Bryman, A., Ford, J., Keil, T., and Beardsworth, A. (1983), 'Information in the labour market: the impact of recession', *Sociology*, 17: pp.260–7.

Jerrome, D. (1981), 'The significance of friendship for women in later life', *Ageing and Society*, 1: pp.175–97.

Jerrome, D. (1984), 'Good company: the sociological implications of friendship', *Sociological Review*, 32: pp.696–718.

Johnson, F. L. and Aries, E. J. (1983), 'The talk of women friends', *Women's Studies International Forum*, 6: pp.353–61.

Klein, J. (1965), *Samples from English Culture*, Routledge & Kegan Paul, London.

Kurth, S. (1970), 'Friendships and friendly relations', in G. McCall (ed), *Social Relationships*, Aldine, Chicago.

Lazarsfeld, P. and Merton, R. (1954), 'Friendship as social process', in M. Berger, T. Abel and C. H. Page (eds), *Freedom and Control in Modern Society*, Van Nostrand, Princeton.

Lee, G. (1985), 'Kinship and social support of the elderly: the case of the United States', *Ageing and Society*, 5: pp.19–38.

Lee, R. M. (1985), 'Redundancy, labour markets and informal relations', *Sociological Review*, 33: pp.469–94.

Lee, S. C. (1964), 'The primary group as Cooley defines it', *Sociological Quarterly*, 5: pp. 23-34.

Leonard, D. (1980), *Sex and Generation: A Study of Courtship and Weddings*, Tavistock, London.

Leslie, L. and Grady, K. (1985), 'Changes in mothers' social networks and social support following divorce', *Journal of Marriage and the Family*, 47: pp.663–73.

Levy, J. A. (1981), 'Friendship dilemmas and the intersection of social worlds', in H. Z. Lopata and D. Maines (eds), *Research in the Interweave of Social Roles: Friendship*, Jai Press, Greenwich, Conn.

Lewin, K. (1948), 'Social-psychological differences between the United States and Germany', in G. W. Lewin (ed), *Resolving Social Conflicts*, Harper & Row, New York.

Lewis C. S. (1960), *The Four Loves*, Geoffrey Bles, London.

Lewis, R. A. (1978), 'Emotional initimacy among men', *Journal of Social Issues*, 34: pp. 108–21.

Leyton, E. (1974), *The Compact*, Newfoundland Social and Economic Papers No. 3, Memorial University of Newfoundland.

Littlejohn, J. (1963), *Westrigg*, Routledge & Kegan Paul, London.

Litwak, E. (1960a), 'Occupational mobility and extended family cohesion', *American Sociological Review*. 25: pp.9–21.

Litwak, E. (1960b), 'Geographic mobility and extended family cohesion', *American Sociological Review*, 25: pp.385–94.

Litwak, E. (1965), 'Extended kin relations in an industrial democratic society', in E. Shanas and G. F. Streib (eds), *Social Structure and the Family*, Prentice Hall, Englewood Cliffs.

Litwak, E. and Szelenyi, I. (1969). 'Primary group structures and their functions: kin, neighbours and friends', *American Sociological Review*, 34: pp.465–81.

Litwak, E. (1985), *Helping the Elderly*, Guilford Press, New York.

Lockwood, D. (1966), 'Sources of variation in working class images of society', *Sociological Review*, 14: pp.249–67.

Lopata, H. Z. (1979), *Women as Widows*, Elsevier, New York.

Lopata H. Z. (1981), 'Friendship: historical and theoretical introduction', in H. Z. Lopata and D. Maines (eds), *Research in the Interweave of Social Roles: Friendship,* Jai Press, Greenwich, Conn.

Lowenthal, M. F. and Haven, C. (1968), 'Interaction and adaptation: intimacy as a critical variable', *American Sociological Review,* pp.20–30.

Lowenthal, M. F., Thurnher, M. and Chiriboga, D. (1975), *Four Stages of Life: A Comparative Study of Women and Men Facing Transitions,* Jossey-Bass, San Francisco.

Maccoby, E. E. and Jacklin, C. N. (1974), *The Psychology of Sex Differences,* Stanford University Press, Stanford, California.

Maclean, M. and Eekelaar, J. (1983), *Children and Divorce: Economic Factors,* Centre for Socio-Legal Studies, Oxford.

Maines, D. R. (1981), 'The organizational and career contexts of friendship amongst postdoctoral students', in H. Z. Lopata and D. Maines (eds), *Research in the Interweave of Social Roles: Friendship,* Jai Press, Greenwich, Conn.

Marsden, D. (1969), *Mothers Alone,* Allen Lane, Harmondsworth.

Marsden, D. and Duff, E. (1975), *Workless,* Penguin, Harmondsworth.

Marsden, D. (1978), 'Sociological perspectives on family violence', in J. P. Martin (ed), *Violence and the Family,* Wiley, Chichester.

Marshall, G. (1984), 'On the sociology of women's unemployment, its neglect and significance', *Sociological Review,* 32: pp.234–59.

Martin, R. and Wallace, J. G. (1984), *Working Women in Recession: Employment, Redundancy and Unemployment,* Oxford University Press, Oxford.

Matthews, S. H. (1983), 'Definitions of friendship and their consequences in old age', *Ageing and Society,* 3: pp.144–55.

Matthews, S. H. (1986), *Friendships Through the Life Course,* Sage, Beverly Hills.

McCall, G. (ed) (1970), *Social Relationships,* Aldine, Chicago.

McKee, L. and Bell, C. (1986), 'His unemployment, her problem: the domestic and marital consequences of male unemployment', in S. Allen, A. Waton, K. Purcell and S. Wood (eds), *The Experience of Unemployment,* Macmillan, Basingstoke.

McKee, L. (1987), 'Households during unemployment: the resourcefulness of the unemployed', in J. Brannen and G. Wilson (eds), *Give and Take in Families: Studies in Resource Distribution,* Allen & Unwin, London.

McKinley, J. B. (1973), 'Social networks, lay consultation and help-seeking behaviour', *Social Forces,* 51: pp.275–92.

Milardo, R. M. (1986), 'Personal choice and social constraint in close relationships: applications of network analysis', in V. J. Derlega and B. A. Winstead (eds), *Friendship and Social Interaction,* Springer-Verlag, New York.

Milardo, R. M. (1987), 'Changes in social networks of women and men following divorce: a review', *Journal of Family Issues,* 8: pp.78–96.

166   Bibliography

Miles, A. (1988), *Women and Mental Illness*, Harvester Wheatsheaf, Hemel Hempstead.
Mitchell, J. C. (ed) (1969), *Social Networks in Urban Situations*, Manchester University Press, Manchester.
Mogey, J. (1956), *Family and Neighbourhood*, Oxford University Press, London.
Morris, L. (1984), 'Patterns of social activity and post-redundancy labour market experience', *Sociology*, 18: pp.339–52.
Naegale, K. (1958), 'Friendship and acquaintances: an exploration of some social distinctions', *Harvard Educational Review*, 28: pp.232–52.
Nissel, M. and Bonnerjea, L. (1982), *Family Care of the Handicapped Elderly: Who Pays?*, Policy Studies Institute, London.
Oakley, A. (1974), *The Sociology of Housework*, Martin Robertson, London.
O'Brien, M. (1987), 'Patterns of kinship and friendship among lone fathers', in C. Lewis and M. O'Brien (eds), *Reassessing Fatherhood*, Sage, London.
Oxley, H. G. (1974), *Mateship and Local Organization*, University of Queensland Press, Brisbane.
Pahl, J. (1983), 'The allocation of money and the structuring of inequality within marriage', *Sociological Review*, 31: pp.237–62.
Pahl, J. (ed) (1985), *Private Violence and Public Policy*, Routledge & Kegan Paul, London.
Pahl, R. E. (1975), *Whose City?*, Penguin, Harmondsworth.
Pahl, R. E. (1984), *Divisions of Labour*, Blackwell, Oxford.
Paine, R. (1969), 'In search of friendship', *Man* (n.s.) 4: pp.505–24.
Paine, R. (1970), 'Anthropological approaches to friendship', *Humanitas*, 6: pp.139–59.
Parker, R. (1981), 'Tending and social policy', in E.M. Goldberg and S. Hatch (eds), *A New Look at the Personal Social Services*, Policy Studies Institute, London.
Parsons, T. (1956), 'The American family: its relations to personality and to the social structure', in T. Parsons and R. F. Bales (eds), *Family: Socialization and Interaction Process*, Routledge & Kegan Paul, London.
Petrowsky, M. (1976), 'Marital status, sex and the social networks of the elderly', *Journal of Marriage and the Family*, 38: pp.749–56.
Pihlblad, C. T. and Adams, D. L. (1972), 'Widowhood, social participation and life satisfaction', *Aging and Human Development*, 3: pp.323–30.
Pitt-Rivers, J. (1961), 'Interpersonal relations in peasant society', *Human Organization*, 19: pp. 180–3.
Platt, J. (1969), 'Some problems in measuring the jointness of conjugal role relationships', *Sociology*, 3: pp. 287–97.
Pleck, J. H. (1976), 'Man to man: is brotherhood possible?', in N. Glazer-Malbin (ed), *Old Family/New Family: Interpersonal Relationships*, Van Nostrand, New York.
Pollert. A. (1981), *Girls, Wives, Factory Lives*, Macmillan, Basingstoke.

Popay, J., Rimmer, L. and Rossiter, C. (1983), *One-Parent Families: Parents, Children and Public Policy*, Study Commission on the Family, London.

Porter, M. (1983), *Home, Work and Class Consciousness*, Manchester University Press, Manchester.

Powers, E. A. and Bultena, G. L. (1976) 'Sex differences in intimate friendships of old age', *Journal of Marriage and the Family*, 38: pp.739–47.

Qureshi, H. and Simons, K. (1987), 'Resources within families: caring for elderly people', in J. Brannen and G. Wilson (eds), *Give and Take in Families: Studies in Resource Distribution*, Allen & Unwin, London.

Rands, M. (1988), 'Changes in social networks following marital separation and divorce', in R. M. Milardo (ed), *Families and Social Networks*, Sage, Newbury Park.

Roberto, K. A. and Scott, J. P. (1986), 'Friendships of older men and women: exchange patterns and satisfaction', *Psychology and Aging*, 1: pp.103–9.

Rosecrance, J. (1986), 'Racetrack buddy relations: compartmentalized and satisfying', *Journal of Social and Personal Relationships*, 3: pp.441–56.

Rosow, I. (1967), *Social Integration of the Aged*, Free Press, New York.

Rosow, I. (1970), 'Old people: their friends and neighbors', *American Behavioural Scientist*, 14: pp.59–69.

Rubin, L. B. (1985), *Just Friends: The Role of Friendship in Our Lives*, Harper & Row, New York.

Rubin, L. B. (1986), 'On men and friendship', *Psychoanalytical Review*, 73: pp.165–81.

Sadler, W. (1970), 'The experience of friendship', *Humanitas*, 6: pp.177–209.

Seiden, A. M. and Bart, P. B. (1976). 'Woman to woman: is sisterhood powerful?', in N. Glazer-Malbin (ed), *Old Family/New Family: Interpersonal Relationships*, Van Nostrand, New York.

Sennett, R. (1980), 'Destructive gemeinschaft', in R. Bocock, P. Hamilton, K. Thompson and A. Waton (eds), *An Introduction to Sociology*, Fontana, London.

Sharpe, S. (1984), *Double Identity*, Penguin, Harmondsworth.

Sinfield, A. (1981), *What Unemployment Means*, Martin Robertson, London.

Spanier, G. B. and Casto, R. F. (1979), 'Adjustment to separation and divorce', *Journal of Divorce*, 2: pp.241–53.

Stacey, M. (1960), *Tradition and Change*, Oxford University Press, London.

Stacey, M., Batstone, E., Bell, C. and Murcott, A. (1975), *Power, Persistence and Change*, Routledge & Kegan Paul, London.

Suitor, J. (1987), 'Friendship networks in transitions: married mothers' return to school', *Journal of Social and Personal Relationships*, 4: pp.445–61.

Suttles, G. (1970), 'Friendship as a social institution', in G. McCall (ed), *Social Relationships*, Aldine, Chicago.

Tiger, L. (1969), *Men in Groups*, Random House, New York.

Toomey, D.M. (1971), 'Conjugal roles and social networks in an urban working class sample', *Human Relations*, 24: pp.417–31.

Unruh, D. R. (1983), *Invisible Lives*, Sage, Beverly Hills.

Wallace, C. (1987), *For Richer, For Poorer: Growing Up In and Out of Work*, Tavistock, London.

Warr, P. (1983), 'Work, jobs and unemployment', *Bulletin of the British Psychological Society*, 36: pp. 305–11.

Watson, W. (1964), 'Social mobility and social class in industrial communities', in M. Gluckman and E. Devons (eds), *Closed Systems and Open Minds*, Oliver & Boyd, Edinburgh.

Wellman, B. (1985), 'Domestic work, paid work and net work', in S. Duck and D. Perlman (eds), *Understanding Personal Relationships*, Sage, Beverly Hills.

Wenger, G. C. (1984), *The Supportive Network: Coping with Old Age*, Allen & Unwin, London.

Westwood, S. (1984), *All Day, Every Day: Factory and Family in the Making of Women's Lives*, Pluto, London.

Whitehead, A. (1976), 'Sexual antagonism in Herefordshire', in D. L. Barker and S. Allen (eds), *Dependence and Exploitation in Work and Marriage*, Longman, London.

Wilkin, D. (1979), *Caring for the Mentally Handicapped Child*, Croom Helm, London.

Williams, R. G. A. (1981), 'The art of migration', *Sociological Review*, 29: pp.621–47.

Williams, R. G. A. (1983), 'Kinship and migration strategies among settled Londoners', *British Journal of Sociology*, 34: pp.386–415.

Williams, W. M. (1956), *The Sociology of an English Village: Gosforth*, Routledge & Kegan Paul, London.

Willis, P. (1977), *Learning to Labour*, Saxon House, Farnborough.

Willmott, P. (1963), *The Evolution of a Community: A Study of Dagenham After Forty Years*, Routledge & Kegan Paul, London.

Willmott, P. (1966), *Adolescent Boys of East London*, Routledge & Kegan Paul, London.

Willmott, P. (1987), *Friendship Networks and Social Support*, Policy Studies Institute, London.

Wiseman, J. P. (1986), 'Friendship: bonds and binds in a voluntary relationship', *Journal of Social and Personal Relationships*, 3: pp.191–211.

Wolf, E. R. (1966), 'Kinship, friendship and patron-client relations in complex societies', in M. Banton (ed), *The Social Anthropology of Complex Societies*, Tavistock, London.

Wood, V. and Robertson, J. F. (1978), 'Friendship and kinship interaction: differential effect on the morale of the elderly', *Journal of Marriage and the Family*, 40: pp.367–75.

Wright, P. H. (1982), 'Men's friendships, women's friendships and the alleged inferiority of the latter', *Sex Roles*, 8: pp.1–20.

Yeandle, S. (1984), *Women's Working Lives: Patterns and Strategies*, Tavistock, London.

Young, M. and Willmott, P. (1957), *Family and Kinship in East London*, Routledge & Kegan Paul, London.

INDEX